The Mario Lanza Story

The
Mario Lanza Story

BY

CONSTANTINE CALLINICOS
WITH RAY ROBINSON

Illustrated

We fooles that gaze on great ones and admire
Their outward light, feele not their inwarde fire.
Our eyes behold them followed and attired
Like Gods on earth; but were our minds inspired
To see them when these clouds are overblowne,
They are but wretches when they are alone

—ANONYMOUS

Contents

The Mario Lanza Story

1. Three Days in London

*I*T LASTED for three days and three nights—this terrible affliction of my friend, Mario Lanza. It turned him into an uncontrollable, irrational thing. There was no reasoning with him, no steering him from his course of self-destruction. There was no plea that could win back his senses or his large heart.

With time out only for exhaustion, he drank champagne steadily for 72 hours. I'll never forget that binge as long as I remember Mario. . . .

Two weeks before, when both of us were in Rome, Mario had been in one of his moods of depression and restlessness. Then I received his phone call. I could hear the sudden excitement in his voice, and immediately I knew something important had happened to him—something, perhaps, that might serve to restore his confidence and well-being.

"Costa," he said, almost singing it out, "we're going to sing a Command Performance before the Queen of England."

"That's wonderful," I answered. "You'll be great!"

"You're damn right I'll be great," Mario exploded. "I'll sing like those British have never heard anyone sing before!"

Mario's agents—General Artists in New York and Leslie Grade in London—had informed him that the Command Performance was set for Monday night, November 18, 1957, at the Palladium, London's most famous music hall. All proceeds would go to the Variety Artists' Benevolent Fund. It would be Mario's first concert engagement since the windup of his tumultuous *Great Caruso* tour in Fresno, California, six years before.

As the time came to leave for London, Mario acted like a boy again, and Betty, his wife, shared his excitement. On the train he told us how well his records and his movies had done in England. His concert there was sure to be a big success.

"Let's drink to it!" Mario said as the Golden Arrow pulled slowly into London's Victoria Station. We joined him in two glasses of wine, and when Mario turned to stare out of the window at the crowd, I looked at Betty for a long moment, hopefully.

As Mario stepped off the train he was engulfed in a sea of screaming women—teenagers to dowagers. Carrying banners hastily scrawled WELCOME MARIO, they broke *en masse* through the platform barriers set up by the police.

I tried to stay close to Mario, but he disappeared in the maelstrom. Some women embraced him, others tried to kiss him. They finally succeeded in knocking him off his feet.

Dazed but beaming, Mario picked himself up and sought refuge in one of the coaches of the Golden Arrow. I followed him. Mario's tie was gone—a souvenir for a fan—and his suit was crumpled. But he was happy.

"This is my first good breath in ten minutes," he said. "But who cares! This is great. When they stop doing this, you're out of business."

That was Thursday evening, November 14—an exciting occasion. What followed was a nightmare.

The binge began soon after Mario reached the Dorchester Hotel. A press conference had been arranged by Leslie Grade, in charge of all those little things presumed to make the life of a celebrity comfortable. In the past, reporters had been deprecatory and sometimes unfair and cruel to Mario, who thrived on affection and adulation. Spited to his face and in the public prints, Mario resorted to the one meager weapon that he possessed in any battle of wits: scurrility. And the correspondents implied as much in their stories.

So, as the reporters trooped into his luxurious suite, Mario started to fortify himself for another ordeal. I saw him down a glass of champagne. Then a second. He seemed to anticipate disaster. But by drinking he made disaster inescapable. I prayed quietly to myself that the session would be a mild one, that the questions would be a little kind and thoughtful.

My hopes were shredded quickly.

"What do you weigh these days?" asked a reporter, forfeiting his rights to originality.

Mario, who had once isolated himself from his friends out of self-consciousness, was stung by the question. He glared at the reporter, then fumed and exploded. "For God's sake, isn't there anything else you people can ask an artist?" shouted Mario.

I knew the torrent and torment had started—all over again. Mario blustered, stormed and raged through the rest of the press conference.

He felt that he was being provoked and needled for his weakness; he felt they were laughing at him. His mind, now befogged by champagne, was a cavern of self-pity, a seething ferment of paranoia.

The next day there were the newspaper reports. Though they were more objective than I thought they would be, the usual barbs were present.

"The tubby, temperamental tenor," or the man with "the King Farouk silhouette" was the way they characterized him. And they could say in all truth that he "uses expletives like punctuation marks."

Mario read these sarcasms—and drank more. Why did his travels always have to be documented with talk of weight, eating, special diets, gluttony? It hadn't been a circus freak who had just arrived in London. It had been Mario Lanza, the singer. He was not a whale on a flatboat.

All day Mario drank. Strictly champagne.

He drank alone. He drank with friends, waiters—anyone who wandered into his suite.

"It'll stop tomorrow," I said to Betty.

"It has to," she said.

I went to Mario. "You have to pull yourself together," I said to him. "For God's sake, stop this insane drinking and let's get the voice in shape."

"*You* better go and rehearse the orchestra," was his answer. "I'll be all right Monday."

It did not stop the next day—Saturday. The rehearsal day was lost. Knowing Mario would not appear, I went to the Palladium anyway. In front of the stage door hundreds of people were lined up to see Mario arrive for his rehearsal. The British bobbies were out in force to protect him upon his arrival. The crowds and the bobbies waited all day long. And Mario never came. With heavy heart, I rehearsed the orchestra and returned to the hotel.

Mario did the impossible that Saturday. He drank more than I had ever seen him drink before, and few men have the capacity for drink that Mario possessed.

Early Sunday morning I went to Mario's hotel room. I was determined to stop him before he destroyed himself in full view of all of us. Only one day—24 hours—separated Mario from his appearance before the Queen. It was still possible for Mario, a man with the physical strength of a bull, to rebound from his binge. But he had to stop immediately!

A waiter, cuddling a chilled bottle of champagne, preceded me into the suite. As I entered, my heart sank.

Mario stood uncertainly in the center of the room in his blue dressing gown. His face was red, puffy, and unshaven, and his eyes seemed to have difficulty focusing on me. The dead magnums of champagne surrounded him—so many miserable relics of his personal battlefield. I remembered that Mario always insisted the bottles be removed as soon as he had emptied them. That so many magnums were lying about could mean only that Mario was drinking faster than the waiters were disposing of the evidence. And it was only ten o'clock in the morning.

Peter Pritchard, one of Mario's London agents, who had been watching this tragi-comic performance helplessly, left his seat by the fireplace and walked to my side. "I can't do anything with him," he said in a low voice. "Maybe you can stop him."

Obviously Pritchard knew little about Mario's case history. When Mario reached this point, nothing in the whole world could stop him but himself.

"I'll see what I can do," I said, almost desperately.

As I spoke, another waiter came in with another magnum, received his five-pound tip, and departed. At that rate I could scarcely expect any waiter to forget Mario's room number.

Then Mario caught my eye. "Costa," he blurted out. "Let's go over some songs. We're singing tomorrow night."

Perhaps I should have been grateful that Mario recalled his appointment with the Queen of England. But the idea of fulfilling it was becoming more and more inconceivable. I could feel the anger mounting in me.

"Have a drink, Costa," Mario said huskily. "Have a drink. Join the party."

"No, Mario."

Mario managed to fill a glass and pushed it across the piano toward me. "Here, drink up. *La vita e breve, la morte vien*," he said, with a dramatic flourish. I had heard him utter this phrase—life is brief, death is coming—so often in the past that I had scarcely paid attention to it. But now, suddenly, it became meaningful and portentous to me.

"I don't want any," I said harshly.

"All, right, then let's sing," said Mario.

Thereupon he launched into a barroom version of "Because You're Mine," one of the songs that he had made famous in the movies and on records. Still another waiter, who had just entered the room, looked respectful but puzzled. He knew he was listening to the world-famous Lanza in person, at close range, yet he could not believe it was good. In fact, it was so unbelievably bad, so disgustingly distorted, that I shuddered.

When the song had reached its rasping conclusion, Mario refilled a glass for himself and approached me. "That wasn't so bad," he said. "It'll be fine tomorrow night. Don't worry, Costa."

"Don't worry!" I said incredulously.

"No. You're always worrying about nothing."

"You make me sick!" I shouted, snatching my glass from the piano and flinging it toward the fireplace half a room away. Then I stamped out into the hallway, overwhelmed with anger and helplessness.

In a few minutes I was walking aimlessly around Hyde Park. When I came to the Serpentine, a large lake in the center of the park, I vaguely recalled a story I had once heard about the poet Shelley's first wife, Harriet Westbrook, who had drowned herself in this lake. I was in that kind of black mood.

I heard later from Pritchard that when I slammed the door on Mario he flew into a rage.

"Send that damn Greek back on the first plane," he yelled. "Who the hell does he think he is, talking to me like that!"

I had seen many of Mario Lanza's outbursts, and I knew how frightening, how tragic they were. All Pritchard could do was wait for it to subside. When it did, Mario started to cry, terrible sobs that wracked his whole body.

A waiter knocked at the door tentatively, observed Mario in a heap on the couch, delivered his champagne, and hurried out. For a moment Mario stared at the champagne through bleary eyes. Then he got up and walked into the bedroom, out of sight of Pritchard.

If it was something I had said or done, I will never know. But something—fatigue, shame, disgust with himself, physical pain— had broken through to him. Mario had at last stopped drinking.

At two o'clock that Sunday afternoon he fell asleep.

Early Monday morning the phone rang shrilly in my room. It was Mario's voice on the other end. Miraculously the huskiness was gone. There was spirit and exultation in it.

"Don't worry," Mario said. There it was again, the same old reassurance that I had heard too often. "We'll do a good show to-night."

"Are you feeling all right?" I asked.

There was a painful pause. Then Mario said, "Yes. Thanks for everything."

2. Command Performance

$\mathcal{L}$ONDON'S 2,500-seat Palladium, plush, cavernous and crimson, with marble pillars and a stage large enough to present a circus, has long been a showcase for the great talents of the entertainment world. From the moment I heard Mario was to sing there at the Royal Variety Show for the Queen, I thought of it as an opportunity for him to purge himself of his private demons. I kept hoping it would restore meaning and tranquillity to his life. But knowing how sick Mario was, I knew I was asking for a miracle.

The years after the tremendously successful *Great Caruso* tour had been destructive; they had been years of tempest, trial, and self-inflicted torment. Mario's fantastic overindulgence in food and drink, his emotional tirades, his canceled commitments, his wild eccentricities, had ruined his career; but now, with perhaps his last chance, Mario had succumbed again to his compulsive thirst. The bitterness I felt was surpassed only by my sympathy for him. I still felt he could recover physically from the results of his three-day binge, but I did not think he would ever have the desire or confidence to sing in public again.

Yet there he was, sobered if exhausted, decked out in his tuxedo, standing in his dressing room at the Palladium, waiting nervously to go on. His friends and business associates—Bill Judd of Columbia Artists Management in New York, John Coast, Columbia Management representative in London, Leslie Grade—were on hand. If they were aware of the weekend struggle that had taken place, certainly nobody in the Palladium audience was.

Mario tried to joke with me. "Did you ever see so many bobbies in your life? They haven't forgotten me."

The bobbies were on hand primarily to protect Queen Elizabeth and Prince Philip. But I was glad to let Mario stake his claim.

He started to sing a few lines, testing the voice he had mistreated so unmercifully. It didn't sound too bad. He asked me to mouth the lyrics of his three selections as I conducted the orchestra so that he could cue himself if his memory failed during the performance. The fear of forgetting his lyrics eternally haunted Mario, as it has so many other singers.

We could hear noise rise outside, a sure sign the Queen's party had arrived. Then the British National Anthem was played. The show had officially started.

One by one the entertainers went on; all of them, including the popular Gracie Fields, were British. I knew the suspense was unbearable for Mario.

Then finally his name was announced. There was a reassuring roar of applause from the audience: they hadn't forgotten him. But as he walked across the stage, Mario was terribly alone with his thoughts and anxieties.

The blazing spotlight focused on him now. A trickle of moisture formed on his forehead. I could only hope he would get through it. Give Mario courage! Help him remember the words! I looked up at him from the orchestra pit, smiling confidently as I always tried to do during our concerts.

I tapped my baton. The music began. Mario started to sing "Because You're Mine."

The tones—orotund and bold—filled the Palladium. It was not Mario at his best, but I was willing to settle for it. After his first song, then after "Loveliest Night of the Year" and "E lucevan le stelle," the crowd expressed its approval in thunderous applause.

At the end, his ordeal finished, Mario stood, sweat streaking down his face in rivulets. He absorbed the roar of the crowd like a sponge. He took endless bows, acknowledging me in the conductor's pit. Then he walked off, a man who had defied all the odds and won some sort of victory.

Afterward, to escape the autograph seekers, we had dinner at an out-of-the-way restaurant. But they still found Mario, and he grinned and signed happily. Mario always welcomed his fans. He may have had his moments of rudeness and boorishness, but the people who bought and loved his records and flocked to his movies were never subjected to it.

"I feel wonderful," Mario cried. "I'd like to sing all over the world now."

I am an eternal optimist. My faith in Mario had been shattered repeatedly, but I wanted to believe what he said. And as I listened to Mario picture another triumphant tour of America, I began to believe what I wanted to—that he had indeed passed the crisis.

I was wrong again.

3. One Night in Shippensburg

I FIRST met Mario Lanza in New York in 1947, just ten years before the ordeal at the Palladium. At the time, I was enjoying a two-week break in the rigors of coping with capricious prima donnas, living out of suitcases, and eating-grindingly fast-greasy meals.

One morning I received a call from Zena Hanenfeldt of Columbia Artists Management.

"How would you like to play a date at Shippensburg, Pennsylvania?" she asked me.

"Never heard of the place," I said mournfully.

"You'd be playing for a tenor named Mario Lanza."

"Never heard of him, either."

"You will," she assured me.

Then the details of the financial arrangements were outlined to me—Lanza was working for a "small" fee and I was to receive a "small cut" from that. I became less interested by the second, but after she hung up something prompted me to dial Lanza's number.

In those days Mario lived at 8 West 49th Street, an old apartment building overlooking Rockefeller Plaza. Mario and his wife Betty liked to call the place "The Bohemian Garret."

Mario answered the phone and began discussing the concert in his exuberant, friendly manner. I had the sudden impression that I had known him all my life.

"When do you like to rehearse?" I asked him.

"We don't need to rehearse. I've got other things to do." There was a pause. Then: "I have confidence in you, Constantine."

Considering I'd never set eyes on the man, it was an extraordinary conversation. Considering, too, that he was a neophyte with only a limited repertoire, including a handful of arias, concert standards and semiclassical operettas, it was an astonishing approach to his work.

We decided to rendezvous in Shippensburg on April 14.

Just two hours before the concert we met in the tiny Pennsylvania town.

"The train runs right through Main Street here," Mario said, his brown eyes sparkling as he shook my hand. He was just twenty-six, with a fresh, simple, ingenuous vigor that I had rarely seen before among professional artists. He had the build and the barrel chest of a heavyweight fighter, and was in excellent shape. In the first few seconds I had to judge him uncomplicated and unspoiled, a press agent's delight.

But as I was to learn to my sadness, Mario was neither uncomplicated nor unspoiled, but deeply disturbed. As the years went by and I learned more about Mario, the artist and man, I could only marvel at how wrong my first impression had been. Only my genuine fondness for him could have kept me with him through all the trials and turbulences that ensued.

Betty, the girl from Chicago, was a lively brunette of medium height with a trim figure. If Mario looked like a choir boy, she was as wholesome as "the girl next door." There was nothing about them that warned me. There was no sign of the evil star under which they lived out their lives.

Our first concern that carefree day in Shippensburg was a tuxedo—the one that Mario didn't have.

"Let's appear in business suits," said Mario, who loathed formality and artistic pretense as well as rehearsals.

So, wearing business suits, we stepped onto the stage of the State Teachers College auditorium. A good part of the town's population of 5,722 was on hand for the concert, and I hadn't played a single note of Mario's repertoire.

As I started to play the introduction of "Pieta Signore" by Stradella, a favorite of Enrico Caruso's, Mario turned his back on the audience. Leaning casually over the grand piano, he winked, then smiled at me. I had already played, in my budding career, for many famous artists, including Lily Pons and Lauritz Melchior, but it was inconceivable that any of them would have behaved in this fashion. But that was Mario.

Then he began singing, and I knew that the tux was unimportant, and that the offensive, tradition-defying back-to-the-audience was just a neophyte's lack of stage deportment. For as the rich, glorious tones flowed effortlessly from Mario's throat, I knew I was listening to one of. the greatest tenor voices since Caruso. Through Mario's vocal chords, and through those bony cavities in his throat, nose and mouth which are called the resonators, emerged phrases of such opulence, warmth and velvety quality that I sat there feeling some incredible joke had been played on me. The notes were round and lush, satisfying and meaningful, and his breath control, on the long phrases, was truly amazing.

Each selection he approached with relish and enthusiasm. He seemed able to communicate his depth of feeling for each song. It was only a matter of minutes before he had the audience in the palm of his hand, applauding and cheering him to the echo.

Then I noticed another peculiar trait—peculiar, that is, to our profession. After taking a bow at the end of each group of selections, he walked insouciantly to the wing of the stage, where Betty waited for him with a glass of water. He sipped the water slowly while the crowd prolonged its applause. He was in no hurry to get back to acknowledge the acclaim. Each time he let the hypnotized audience wait upon him. Any other artist would have taken at least five bows during this ovation.

Now, when I reflect on the incident, I realize that the glass of water was characteristic: while Mario drank from it he was making the public wait, he was letting things ride, he was procrastinating. That day, Mario had inadvertently shown me the pattern of his whole life and career—except in years to come it was not with water that he spited himself and the realities of the moment.

After the concert we went for a midnight snack to a little restaurant across the street from the assembly hall, and I had some time to begin to know Mario.

He was delighted over the success of the evening, but my excitement was considerably greater than his. For that night I had become a partner of a man whose voice was the most prodigious I had ever heard.

"Mario, Mario, what a voice!" I exclaimed.

"You haven't heard anything yet," Mario laughed.

Our sandwiches and coffee could not have come to more than $3, but as we got up to leave, Mario tipped the waitress two dollars. After paying his agent and me and deducting his transportation expenses, Mario would have little left of his modest fee. When Betty reminded him of that he laughed. "Hell, it's only money," he said.

At the time I thought that the man with the biggest voice in the world was also the man with the most generous heart.

4. Freddy Becomes Mario

FROM time to time during his career, Mario, largely depending on the mood of the moment, would dispute his studio, his press agents, his friends, and even his own mother and father as to the exact date and place of his birth.

In the last years of his life, when Betty and he moved with their family of four children—Colleen, Elissa, Damon and Marc—to Rome, he often insisted to anyone who would listen that he was certainly *not* born in January, 1921, in Philadelphia, as most stories said.

"The studio wanted me to say that I was born in 1921," Mario would explain, "because that was the year Caruso died. They figured it was a good gimmick, one of those startling coincidences. But it was strictly a lot of bunk. I was really born in 1925, in New York."

In truth, Mario was actually born as Alfredo Arnold Cocozza on January 31, 1921, in South Philadelphia, in a district that was popularly known as Little Italy though it had a profusion of Irish. And 1921 was, as a matter of fact and history, the year the unforgettable Caruso died, at the age of forty-eight, in his home town of Naples.

Why Mario fought the record book, I could only guess. Partly he was exercising his right to be capricious. Partly he enjoyed giving members of the press misinformation just to see if they would publish it. But principally, I think, he was trying to deny and at the same time emphasize the constant comparison of Mario Lanza to Enrico Caruso.

The first time I had a chance to talk to Mario at great length he also insisted that as a youth of seven or eight he had watched a Mafia-type killing of one of his close relatives.

"They came and knocked him off right on our doorstep, and I was there to see the blood flow down the street. Then I ran like hell," Mario told me. As I became familiar with Mario's desire to dramatize his early life, I discounted this tale as just another good story. However, I have since learned that such an event actually did occur during Mario's boyhood.

Both of Mario's parents were born in Italy. Antonio Cocozza, Mario's father, was a native of Filignano and came to the United States when he was twelve years old. Maria, his mother, was born in Abruzzi and arrived in America when she was just past six months of age.

As a youngster Tony Cocozza loved to ride bikes and listen to opera. Before World War I he was known as one of the best cyclists around Philadelphia; on one occasion he came to New York and rode in Madison Square Garden. Ironically, Tony's first job in America was shellacking cabinets for RCA Victor, a corporation that some years later was to reap substantial rewards from the golden voice of Tony's son. Later, Tony ran a lathe machine, trimming iron for locomotive parts. He had an amateurish addiction to the French horn.

In World War I, Tony fought in the Battle of the Meuse-Argonne as a member of the 37th Division, 145th Infantry. One day he captured a German prisoner but shortly after that he was seriously wounded by German dumdum bullets, which grotesquely shattered the lower part of his right arm. This wound, together with his earlier gassing and back wound, ended his Army career and made him, in civilian life, an ambulatory invalid on a total disability pension.

Still nursing his wounds, Tony entered a Philadelphia grocery store one afternoon in 1919 to purchase some Italian salami. Maria Lanza, a dark-haired, delicate-featured girl of sixteen, was behind the counter. Tony, still in his Army uniform, stopped to talk to Maria—and forgot about the salami. Barely six weeks later they were married.

In 1921, Alfredo—always Freddy to his parents—was born, at 636 Christian Street, above the grocery store operated by Salvatore Lanza, Maria's father. Salvatore was a good businessman, and though Tony didn't work, the family never had to worry about its next meal.

Maria, who could play the pianola, once hoped for a singing career. But Salvatore wouldn't hear of it: the stage was no place for a married woman to spend her time. So, until Mario's voice started to develop, Tony Cocozza had to content himself with his records of grand opera.

When little Freddy was barely five he showed an intense interest in the old Victrola that Tony Cocozza played night and day in the small dining room. The glorious, robust tones of Caruso, sobbing the heartbroken Canio's lines from *I Pagliacci*, shook the windows but warmed the heart of the only child in the house. Sometimes he would sit for hours and listen to a single record over and over again. One night, when he was just seven, he played *"Vesti la giubba"* over twenty-five times.

The Cocozzas bought at Frank Ianarella's shop all the records they could afford to buy. Maria took odd jobs, as a seamstress in the Philadelphia quartermaster for seven years, as a sample maker for rugs for five years, as a waitress in an ice cream parlor. But she preferred taking in sewing at home, so she could keep her eye on Freddy.

Maria sang to Freddy and he listened with keen attention. When Freddy was eight, Salvatore Lanza, who had seven other children in addition to Maria (and managed to extract the ultimate in obedience from all of them; only "one little squirt," grandson Freddy, talked back to him), decided that he didn't want Maria roaming around Philadelphia on odd jobs. So he gave Tony Cocozza a subsidy to open up a modest candy store in the neighborhood.

However, after two years Tony had to concede for all time that he was not a businessman. It wasn't that the work was too hard for the disabled man. Rather, he was thoroughly incapable of demanding *quid pro quo* from his customers, most of whom were youngsters looking to buy ice cream and candy for themselves, or tobacco and magazines for their parents. He loved the children and would give them things for nothing if they turned their pockets inside out, or just looked at him with sad faces. So the Cocozzas closed down their store.

As a little boy Freddy attended a Catholic school, the St. Mary Magdalene de Pazzo School on Seventh and Montrose. When he was nine his folks moved to 2040 Mercy Street, into a red brick, two-story house, with six small rooms and bath. Later Freddy attended Nare Junior High and Southern High.

The Cocozza house, with its plain white woodwork and flowered wallpaper, was reasonably comfortable and pleasant. It was typical of the houses in the rest of the neighborhood, which had its two rows of identical two-story homes lining both sides of Mercy Street.

In the morning when he got up, Freddy could gaze out of his upstairs window into a cramped backyard and see a lonely black fig tree from Italy—the only one of its kind in the whole neighborhood. When the figs ripened, almost everybody on Mercy Street would visit the Cocozzas to share in the harvest. On some of these occasions Maria would also show her friends the wonderful stock of pure olive oil and cheeses that she kept in her basement. More often than not, she'd give some away, as Tony had done with the candy and ice cream. But it was there to sell, and to provide additional income for the family.

Freddy grew up as an overindulged, overprotected only child. He was inclined to be athletic and played football, basketball and baseball better than the average boy. But he was a lazy student and avoided studying whenever possible; and he became rebellious, defiant, troubled, and troublesome. In later years Mario acknowledged that he must have been a terrible trial to everyone around him.

Freddy, a sturdily built youngster, was winning a certain renown for his prodigious appetite and his fondness for street brawls. He might pick a fight more often than he was picked on; but his appetite was connected to his generosity. "He always shared what he had with the other boys," remembers one store owner on Philadelphia's Vine Street. "Whenever he'd gotten money from his Mom, Dad or Salvatore Lanza to buy something to eat for himself, everybody ate."

His feats as a practical jokester are clearly recalled by friends and associates of his teenage years. He might walk into a candy store, load up his pockets with bubble gum, chocolates, caramels and nuts, then walk out without paying the proprietor. "We called him 'Jesse James,' " remembers Al De Palma, "but he'd usually come around later and dump all of his haul—or most of it—back onto the counter."

De Palma, a stout, good-natured man with a brief mustache, is the self-styled "King of the Hoagies." For almost thirty years, at 6200 Vine Street, he has been selling his hoagies, which are a delectable De Palma version of the popular Italian Hero sandwich. Freddy became one of his best customers when he was sixteen years old. He ate unbelievable quantities of food at De Palma's restaurant and also came to listen to records, which he played on his own portable record player.

One night in 1939, De Palma recalls, a terrible snowstorm cleared the streets. But in walked Freddy, in his navy-blue wool cap and turtleneck sweater. He had his records and record player under his arm and icicles on his nose and chin. Without a word, Freddy walked to the back of the restaurant, settled himself in a warm corner, and started to play his favorite Caruso and Tito Ruffo records. As he sat and listened, tears rolled down his cheeks.

When it was almost 11:30, Al walked to Freddy's side. "I'm closing up now," he said. But Freddy, still weeping quietly, didn't answer. De Palma closed the restaurant for the night. When he returned in the morning he found Freddy asleep, just where he had left him.

"The boy played his records all night, over and over," said De Palma. "Later when I asked him about it he said he had just felt sad and that he found peace in my restaurant. I'll never forget it; it was kinda strange, the whole thing."

Freddy was a great one for accepting dares. More than once he devoured four gigantic hoagies, full of the best Italian cold cuts and peppers, along with five bottles of soft drinks and three banana splits, all at one sitting. Usually Freddy would enter and sing out his demands for Al's food while De Palma would be trying to wait on his other customers. Once when he came in singing in that strident voice of his, Al threw his ice cream dipper at him. But Freddy only howled with delight.

"If you're the King of the Hoagies," he would yell at De Palma, "someday I'm going to be the king of the singers, like Caruso!"

The disbelief that ordinarily greeted Freddy's promise to be another Caruso was quickly modified when somebody heard Freddy singing along with his records. His striking imitations of the great tenor sent shivers up and down the spine.

But Freddy's desire to emulate Caruso (his second hero was another Italian boy named Joseph Paul DiMaggio) did not extend to serious effort. He would play his records and listen interminably and sometimes sing along with them, but that was all.

"Why don't you go to a school to study music?" a friend asked him one day.

"Some day," said Freddy, "I'll be discovered by someone."

As he pined to emerge as a rival to the immortal Neapolitan tenor, Freddy continued to thread a narrow path between high jinks and delinquency. One episode occurred in the thinly populated resort center of Wildwood, on the southern tip of New Jersey some 85 miles from Atlantic City and 90 miles from Philadelphia, where the Cocozzas often visited during the summer. Freddy and Tony Graziano, a school pal from Southern High (who later became a fight manager), talked their way into jobs with the local trolley line. From six in the evening to one in the morning Freddy, the conductor, titillated the passengers by singing out the names of the streets on the route, while Tony worked as motorman.

The days went pleasantly for all concerned until Freddy took an unauthorized, unchartered trip one day. If it was the first paying job Freddy ever held in his life, it also quickly turned into the last ever offered him in Wildwood.

Eventually Freddy received a sharp setback. Shortly before graduation from Southern High he was summarily expelled for "misconduct." A teacher, so the story goes, made a thoroughly reprehensible remark about Freddy's national antecedents. The boy's instant response was a punch that caromed off the teacher's jaw.

The Cocozzas, naturally, were quite crushed by the incident. But in those moments when Tony Cocozza heard his son's stirring duets with Caruso, he had no alternative but to forgive and forget. A boy possessed of such a rare and lovely singing voice had to be someone special, a blessed human being. He could hardly be expected, thought Tony Cocozza, to act the way other boys did, or to be treated the way other boys were treated. Freddy was certainly not a "bad" boy; he was merely different, groping for his way in the world. As far as Tony was concerned, and Maria, too, that way was as the greatest of all opera singers. Tony was convinced, even before Freddy had a single lesson, that he had somehow fathered the next Caruso.

If there was a single early clue to Freddy's behavior, it was his sightless eye. "Freddy had a convulsion when he was a baby," recalls Maria, "and from that time on he was blind in the left eye. In school he could never read the eye charts with his bad eye, and the teachers always told us about it."

Freddy had little to say about the eye, except, occasionally, that it "bothered" him. And after he became Mario Lanza, he stubbornly refused to mention it to anyone but his closest friends. I know no answer to the question of how Freddy's future life and character were influenced by the blindness. However, one may speculate it played a significant role in his sudden changes from great warmth and generosity to intransigent moodiness and blistering volatility.

If Maria's devotion to her son caused her to exempt him from work and responsibilities, she saw nothing wrong in this. Nor did she like to have Freddy helping her with chores around the house; it was not a boy's job, she felt. So Freddy went along singing with Caruso, collecting his horse pictures (as a child he clipped photos and drawings of horses from newspapers and magazines and hoarded them in three big boxes under his bed), and lifting weights for exercise.

Eager for Freddy to obtain the high school diploma denied him at Southern High, Maria arranged for him to attend Lincoln Preparatory, a Philadelphia private school. Although anxious to please his mother, Freddy had no overriding desire to either study or attend classes. So he approached one of the school's officials with what he thought was a perfectly acceptable solution to a rather wearisome problem.

He offered to pay his tuition, if in return he could be assured passing grades in all his subjects and a diploma—all without attending classes. Of course, the school official refused to hear of it. So Freddy had to face life without the diploma.

Freddy continued to tell his pals that someday he would be great and famous, just like Caruso. One day, after telling it to Tony Graziano, he added thoughtfully, "When that day comes, I'll use the name of Mario Lanza. That's my mother's maiden name." It happened that simply, without the help of press agents, promoters, or movie studio wordsmiths. There was a brief moment, a few years later, when Freddy Cocozza almost became "Marco Polo," but his loving admiration for his mother, and his desire to wear her name before the world, made the name Mario Lanza inevitable, once he had thought of it.

Even those who liked Freddy's singing did not seem to take it seriously. But Tony Cocozza did, and finally he told Maria that Freddy should go to a teacher for voice training. Maria laughed happily and informed him that she had had these same hopes for her son for years. She said that she would take a job at the Philadelphia Quartermaster Depot so that they could pay for the lessons.

Freddy was sent to Irene Williams, a former opera singer. Her coaching did little to rouse him from his lethargy, but she knew, after a year and a half of lessons at $5 per lesson, that Freddy was far more than the usual talent. When he could be coaxed away from his home to sing at a students' concert, Philadelphia society ended up considerably more impressed with Freddy than he was with it.

Maria hired Mario Pellizzon to teach her son the Italian he would need to fulfill his grand opera aspirations. Although Freddy never really mastered Italian, or any other foreign language, he ultimately developed a working knowledge of several, including French, German, and Spanish. (He became a particular specialist, however, in Jewish, Italian and Greek curse words during his Hollywood years.)

For years William K. Huff had been one of the patrons of music in Philadelphia, as well as one of the directors of the Philadelphia Forum, a concert course that included the Boston Symphony, under the aegis of Dr. Serge Koussevitzky. Irene Williams decided to use her acquaintance with Huff to introduce Freddy to Koussevitzky, whose magic reputation could help any deserving young artist's career.

Huff informed Miss Williams that he would be able to get Freddy an audition before Dr. Koussevitzky after a concert at Philadelphia's Academy of Music. The boy had never before set foot in the "Grand Old Lady of Locust Street," but he knew that this meeting was important and he didn't tarry or procrastinate.

Arriving on time for the audition, he went backstage with Bill Huff to meet the great conductor. Dressed in pajama pants and in the midst of an alcohol massage, Dr. Koussevitzky asked Huff to take his charge across the hall; an accompanist there would play anything Freddy wanted to sing.

Freddy's choice was "Vesti la giubba," the aria that had thrilled his parents on countless occasions. As he began to sing, Koussevitzky ordered the rubdown to cease, tiptoed across the hall. When Freddy had rendered the last notes of his selection and stood there, red-faced with the excitement and strain, the conductor spoke. "My boy," he said quietly, a slight tremble in his voice, "you have a truly great voice. I insist you come with me to the Berkshires."

Freddy knew something big and great was happening to him. No one knew that his giant step toward success was also to be a giant step toward tragedy.

Early in World War II the Serge Koussevitzky Music Foundation had been granted permission to use the Tanglewood, Massachusetts, estate and music shed to hold a half-dozen concerts by the students of the Berkshire Music Center. An effort was being made to maintain "public morale under existing conditions." In 1942 many singing hopefuls and gifted young musicians (including Leonard Bernstein) had been invited by Dr. Koussevitzky to come to Tanglewood on scholarships, to train and study under ideal conditions.

The students were routed out of their beds early in the morning; their work rarely ceased before nightfall. Freddy, who at this time put into effect his decision to adopt his mother's maiden name, ducked his assignments when he could. But for the first time in his life he was benefiting by exposure to serious, sustained musical training.

Though he found time to drink beer with the stagehands and make jokes about girls, Mario Lanza also left his mark on that festival. On the night of August 7, 1942, he played Fenton in Otto Nicolai's comic-fantastic opera *The Merry Wives of Windsor*. The opera, first produced in Berlin in 1849, was played in English, in three acts and seven scenes.

Noel Straus, the music critic of *The New York Times*, was mightily impressed with Mario and described him as "an extremely talented, if as yet not completely routined student, whose superb natural singing voice has few equals among the tenors of the day in quality, warmth and power." Mario was thrilled.

Columbia Artists liked what they had heard and seen, too. They signed Mario immediately.

Things were happening quickly for the twenty-one-year-old son of Tony and Maria Cocozza; a whole new world was inviting him in, no questions asked. His voice, which could make a teacup tremble across the room, had removed him forever from the little house on Mercy Street, where the unpredictable moods and torments and tempests of his troubled youth had incubated. But Mario's private demons had only begun to flex their muscles.

Suddenly Mario's success was reversed. On January 5, 1943, after appropriate greetings from his Philadelphia draft board, he was inducted into the United States Army.

5. Mario's War

WHEN Corporal Johnny Silver first ran into Private Mario Lanza, 33477918, the hero of Tanglewood looked like a sketch by Sgt. George Baker, the GI artist who created that compassionate figure in khaki, "Sad Sack." Mario had not been cut out to be a soldier. If he had abhorred discipline on the streets of Philadelphia, he had less taste for it now that he was serving his country. For almost every day of his two years in uniform he was rebellious against authority and resentful of the simplest rules and regulations. He ate so much GI food that he had difficulty buckling his belt, and often fulfilled his assignments in a guard squadron without laces in his shoes.

Marfa, Texas, the air base where Mario met Johnny Silver, was full of dust, tumbleweed, and disaffected GIs. It was a place that produced its quota of World War II heroes, too. But both Johnny and Mario doubted that they would ever see action. Sensing that his destiny was to serve out the war as a Special Services noncommissioned officer, Silver, a tiny, 5' 2" ex-burlesque comic (in postwar years he became a featured performer in *Guys and Dolls* and participated in the memorable "Fugue for Tinhorns"), decided to make the best of a bad deal.

Starved for talk about show business, Johnny spent time searching through service records to locate a GI who might qualify to be his buddy. One afternoon, when his eye fell on Tanglewood in the service record of Alfredo Cocozza, he knew he'd found the right man. He sent word for Cocozza to drop into the Special Services office.

The soldier who presented himself to Silver was a sight. As Silver remembers him, "He was a non-saluting, sloppy guy, who must have weighed close to 250 or 260. But there was also something about him that made me like him immediately. He had eyes that sort of gleamed when he talked. He was so far out of uniform he could have been shot for desertion, but he had more charm than all the generals in the Air Force."

Johnny and Mario hit it off from the start. And when Johnny heard Mario sing he couldn't believe his ears. The little corporal thereupon decided he would do all in his power to keep his singing pal at Marfa. And when rumors of overseas shipments began to circulate Johnny acted fast. He informed his superior officers that he was preparing a show for the GIs on the base, that he needed Lanza to help him with the production and serve as its star.

The plan saved Johnny and his sidekick for Marfa for a while. But as time passed and the show did not materialize, the brass began to look at Silver with a jaundiced eye. He himself became a nominee for overseas shipment.

"If you ship me out, you won't have any production," Johnny warned.

Johnny wasn't shipped out; Marfa never saw his show; and Mario became the chaplain's assistant, where he had access to an organ. Johnny played while he sang.

It was then that good luck, in the person of Peter Lind Hayes, the comedian and night club entertainer, struck Marfa's two exemplary soldiers. Hayes, an Air Force staff sergeant, had written a play called *On the Beam* with Frank Loesser (who won no little renown some years later by authoring *Guys and Dolls*). *On the Beam* was playing the Air Force training camp circuit and Hayes was making the rounds looking for talent.

At Marfa, *On the Beam* added Corporal Silver to its cast. And once Johnny was in the show he asked Hayes to put his friend Mario Lanza in, too.

"What can he do?" asked Peter.

"He can chirp," said Johnny, "like nobody you've ever heard. He'll make Caruso sound like a child."

"Okay, when can I hear him?" asked Hayes.

Johnny told the truth: "The guy's got a cold in his throat from the dampness here. He can't sing for a few days."

Hayes shrugged and started to walk off. But Johnny, who was born and raised on the South Side of Chicago, a tough section of town where each day was a challenge, devised a plan. He ran back to the Special Services office, reached into a filing cabinet for an old recording that he had once taped with Jimmy Durante. On the other side of the record was the voice of Frederick Jagel, the Metropolitan Opera tenor. Johnny had recorded it from a radio broadcast.

He showed the record to Hayes. Peter did not notice that the label, which featured the name Mario Lanza on it, looked suspiciously clean and new.

"Let me hear it," said Hayes.

Hayes' eyes popped.

"He's in!" Peter said.

So Johnny and Mario joined the roving cast of *On the Beam*. They both waited nervously for Mario's voice to return. When Hayes' GIs hit Phoenix, Arizona, the hefty private with the "big voice" still hadn't sung a note. Mario had become the mystery of the troupe. Captain Fred Brisson, son of singer Carl Brisson, had the idea that he *couldn't* sing a note. The pressure mounted on Hayes, not to mention Silver. Finally Johnny said, "Mario, you've got to sing for them tonight. You've got to open your mouth quick. They think you're a phony."

"What am I gonna sing?" asked Mario.

"The same thing you sang on that Jagel record."

The number was "E lucevan le stelle" ("When the stars were brightly shining") from Puccini's *Tosca*.

Fortunately, the dry desert air of Arizona had worked wonders with Mario's lungs. As he stood there, his khaki shirt open at the neck, his head thrown back, Silver knew it would be all right. It was, for it was the voice of Mario Lanza, possibly the best voice of any soldier in the world as of that moment.

When Mario completed his aria, Hayes said, "That was great! You sound even better in person."

It was a year later, when Hayes was in New York preparing to go overseas, that he finally learned the truth about Silver's tampering with the Jagel recording. By that time Mario had been medically discharged from the service and was walking around New York in his civilian clothes. The two met in a theater.

"What are you doing out of uniform?" asked Hayes.

"I just got a discharge," said Mario.

"For what?"

"That damn postnasal drip I had back in Texas."

"How do you like that!" said Peter, feigning exasperation. "Here I am, going overseas, and you, a guy who can break me in half with one hand, are fresh out of the Army. That's justice for you."

"Well," said Mario, "since you may get knocked off, I don't want to have anything on my conscience. Remember that record Johnny Silver played for you in Marfa? The voice was Frederick Jagel's!"

"Thanks for telling me," Hayes said. "Now go get run over."

As a member of the *On the Beam* cast, Mario soon was being hailed as the GI Caruso. In a couple of months Mario & Company traveled some 10,000 miles. Most of their appearances were made before appreciative audiences of Air Force cadets.

"He broke them up," recalls Peter Lind Hayes.

The skit that Mario played in was a broad take-off on *Carmen*. Johnny Silver had a part in it; so did the dancer Ray McDonald, and Jerry Adler, brother of the famed harmonica player Larry Adler.

The setting was a typical Army barrack. As McDonald and Adler mopped the floor, Mario came on, an Army blanket draped over his shoulders and his hat worn sideways, toreador style. Then came Silver, and all four arranged their mop handles into simulated prison bars, vertically and parallel with each other. As the lights dimmed, Mario tried to bash down the brooms, while launching into a spirited version of the bullfighter aria from *Carmen*.

It was the kind of robust theatrics that fitted Mario's talents and temperament perfectly. He enjoyed hearing the GIs roar at his antics and express honest awe at his mighty, uninhibited voice.

Within a few months Moss Hart, who had written a special story, part spectacle, part morality play, about the Air Force, was rounding up talent with the help of Irving Lazar. Mario's voice, already celebrated in Air Force circles, won him a niche in the 50-man choral group.

In all, over 300 men and 42 women were chosen from the Air Force to participate in the staging of the play, which was to be called *Winged Victory*. Hart and Lazar had selected an astonishingly talented group of young actors to appear in the show, and although Mario's reputation, just a half-dozen years later, at least equaled that of any other performer, he was currently just a small, well-fed cog in the machine.

Names from motion pictures and show business dotted the cast: Red Buttons, Barry Nelson, Edmond O'Brien, Alan Baxter, Gary Merrill, George Reeves (who later became famous as "Superman," then committed suicide), Bobby and Billy Mauch (child stars of *The Prince and the Pauper*), Karl Malden, Ray Middleton, Mark Daniels, and Don Taylor. There was also an actor named Bert Hicks, whose sister Betty was to become Mario's wife. They were all thorough troupers, and most of them were working at enlisted man's pay. Each week during the play's run, their efforts produced $25,000 for the Army Emergency Relief Fund.

Hart's story, about the dreams, yearnings, heartbreaks, triumphs, failures, loyalties and simple needs of the brave youngsters learning to fly the B-17s, and B-24s, was a "wonderful show," according to Lewis Nichols of *The New York Times*. But Abel Green of *Variety* came close to what Hart had intended: "It's not a play, but a symbol."

In the play, Mario appeared as one member of a well-balanced chorus under the direction of Lt. Leonard DePaur. Though he was as close to anonymity as a man can get, he became known as "that boy with the tremendous voice." Only Moss Hart himself was unaware of him.

After dress rehearsal in Boston's Shubert Theater (*Winged Victory* opened in New York's 44th Street Theater on November 20, 1943, and played through May 20, 1944), Hart worked frantically on some last-minute changes. By four in the morning most of the cast had left, and Hart had moved to the lounge to rest.

The card games started, then the crap games—then the voice of Mario Lanza.

"I was sitting there, tired and bone-weary," Moss Hart says, "when suddenly, breaking into my early-morning, pre-first-night gloom, was this glorious voice singing 'Celeste Aida' as I had never heard it sung before. I got up and went downstairs to the lounge to locate the man and the voice. I was told it was Mario Lanza.

"I had no idea such a voice was hidden in the chorus. I'd been too busy with the problems of production and direction to pay much attention to the musical background.

"I walked up to him and asked, 'Where did you learn to sing like that?' "

For once Mario's boyish braggadocio facade failed him. He was shy for the moment, and Moss Hart was touched.

"I chatted with him for a while," Hart remembers, "captivated by his childlike innocence. He was outgoing, a darling fellow. The seeds of the destruction were there, but not on the surface."

The experience in *Winged Victory* brought recognition and new associations to Mario. He liked being with such zestful, ambitious, talented and sophisticated young men. And, for the most part, those around him returned the compliment. But, corpulent and round-faced in those months with *Winged Victory*, he became the butt of many a joke; his feats as a trencherman became standard conversation pieces among his buddies.

Mario was hurt and resentful and reacted violently. Once he wandered, foggy-eyed and rubber-legged, into Lieutenant Bill Cahan's dispensary, set up in the rear of the theater. As Cahan approached him, Mario fell into a faint. When Cahan was finally able to revive him, he learned that Mario had not eaten for almost ten days.

"My mother and father are coming down from Philadelphia tomorrow to see the show," Mario tried to explain, "and I didn't want them to see me looking so fat."

Cahan, who has since become a distinguished surgeon in New York City, spent a full year as medical officer to the rambunctious *Winged Victory* cast; seven months while the play packed them in in New York, five months in Hollywood, while a movie version of the play was being made by 20th Century-Fox.

Mario became one of Lieutenant Cahan's favorites. But the doctor was troubled and even fascinated by Mario's mountainous appetite. Cahan had a theory that Mario's weight problem might conceivably be related to his metabolism. So he invited Mario to partake in a little experiment.

For several days Mario was kept in bed and daily blood tests were taken. He had complete confidence in Dr. Cahan, but in the end his superstitious nature won out. He became fearful that he was losing entirely too much blood.

On the fourth morning of the tests Mario, who had been severely limiting his intake of food during this period, suddenly rebelled. He ordered a 23-egg omelette for breakfast and downed it with great gusto, as his friend Barry Nelson looked on. The experiment, of course, ceased with the breakfast.

When the play hit the six-month mark in New York, a party was scheduled for all the members of the cast at the Astor Roof. The night of the party a woman fainted during a performance of the show; Dr. Cahan tended to her needs in the dispensary, then sent her home.

But somehow a story started to make the rounds that the woman really was pregnant, and that Cahan was about to preside over a backstage birth.

When Cahan got wind of the rumor he decided to play along with it. A soldier was quickly dispatched to the dispensary and stretched out on a table under a lady's fur coat. A guard was posted at the door, which now and then would open slightly so the curious could peer in and see the border of the fur coat, with toes protruding.

Before long, the story of Cahan's emergency swept the theater. Then it swept the Astor Roof, where the actors started to assemble for their big blowout.

Halfway through the party Bill Cahan appeared, looking ragged and drawn.

"I have an announcement to make," he began. And everybody, anticipating the nature of it, started to applaud. Cahan held up his arms for silence.

"A little baby boy was born today at our theater," he said with just the proper amount of reverence in his voice. And as everyone burst out in a rousing ovation, a burly figure, completely naked except for a tiny white diaper held on by a huge safety pin, toddled out of the wings toward the center of the Astor stage. He had a lollipop in his mouth and a spit curl on his forehead, and his wailing and screeching rose over the roar of laughter.

The "newborn babe" was Mario, of course.

If Cahan had a warm feeling for Mario, there were others in the cast-among them Edmond O'Brien, Barry Nelson, and Bert Hicks—who shared it. Hicks' relationship with Mario brought Betty Hicks into Mario's life; Betty married Mario about a year after *Winged Victory* was produced in Hollywood.

"Mario loved to come up to Scarsdale," says Eddie O'Brien, the actor's actor who once specialized in Shakespearean roles, "to sing Irish songs for my mother. But the most fun we ever had was when we went to Tony's Restaurant."

The proprietor of Tony's was a man who loved good music. But he had the mistaken impression that he was blessed with a fine voice. Each time they ate there, Mario and O'Brien asked him about his singing; always he accommodated them with an aria. Finally Mario, still protesting his lack of talent, was persuaded to try a song. He imitated the proprietor, croaked out a number.

"My boy, you have no talent, no voice," said the man at Tony's. Then, as he started to leave the table, Mario began to sing.

"It was like one of those scenes from a movie, where the guy or girl starts a song, and everybody crowds around to listen," recalls O'Brien.

The proprietor may have been embarrassed by the joke, but he was also pleased, for the restaurant sold a lot of steaks that day.

When *Winged Victory* moved to Hollywood to be made into a film, under the direction of George Cukor, practically the same cast went with it. For the first time Mario was in Hollywood, the city of flummery and fanfare, which was soon to rocket him to international fame and then to shatter him irreparably.

Though discipline in the outfit was lax, he was in trouble from time to time. One day during the shooting of the movie, Mario was in the background of a scene. When work was halted for the day, he and the others were to be on the set in exactly the same places the next day so that the scene could be accurately completed.

The next day Mario didn't show up. Though he was unimportant to the scene, he was conspicuous by his absence. There was a good deal of frantic searching and hot tempers on set. Blithely Mario showed up for work 48 hours late, none the worse for wear. It was a mischievous, irresponsible, compulsive pattern that was to become accentuated over the next few years.

When he wasn't working on the movie, Mario liked to visit Doris Nelson's tiny Rhapsody Record Shop on North Highland Avenue in Hollywood, and to sing, for nothing, on Friday nights at the Masquer's Club, where actors often assembled. As Mario bellowed his songs in the Rhapsody Record Shop, crowds collected outside and business came to a halt. Onlookers often noticed that the soldier had been drinking.

Many times, hung over and depressed, Mario would sit for hours in the shop, stare into space, and listen to a Gigli or a Caruso record. A sixteen-year-old girl named Patty Orth came to the shop, too, those days. She had the makings of a good mezzo-soprano. Mario became fond of her and her natural talents and wanted to assist her with her singing. In return, Patty became an attentive admirer of Mario and a consolation in his periods of despondency.

However, the budding career that Mario tried to help and encourage came to a tragic end when Patty Orth developed deafness.

Meanwhile the Hollywood celebrities were battling to invite him to their homes. When he came, he never disappointed. Sometimes he would sing nonstop for seven or eight hours. One night, in the home of Frank Sinatra, they cried for more until dawn, and he obliged. Another night, in the home of actress Irene Manning, on North Knoll Drive, he used Walter Pidgeon as his accompanist and serenaded over 75 people, including Edgar Bergen, Atwater Kent, Jimmy Fidler, Reginald Gardiner, and agent Art Rush.

When Mario, his tieless throat throbbing and his fifty-inch chest partially bared to an admiring audience, finished with *Pagliacci*, Rush showered him with compliments and asked him the question he'd been hearing since his Philadelphia days: "Where the devil did you learn to sing?"

"I just kept listening to records," Mario answered happily. If some celebrities considered him ludicrous, for the moment he was buoyant and enthused and damned if he cared what they thought.

Rush, who couldn't quite believe his ears, asked his hostess, "Do you mind if I do a little business here?"

"Go right ahead," Irene said.

Thus, even before Uncle Sam had released him, Mario, with Rush's help, signed an RCA Victor contract for a bonus of $3,000. It was the beginning of a bonanza for RCA.

Always generous to a fault with money, Mario would have had little trouble divesting himself of his new-found wealth. But with the help of a young singer named George London he had no trouble at all. The $3,000 brought a great deal of happiness to waiters, restaurateurs, cab drivers and pretty girls.

"I was at an ice cream counter of a bowling alley in Los Angeles," London says, "and Mario came in and started to count off his money in ten-dollar bills. He lined the bills up on the counter for everybody to see. Then in the next few days we saw to it that it was spent, at places like Ciro's, Mocambo, and Romeo's. As the partial recipient of Mario's windfall, I was grateful. But he really seemed to have an insane impulse to spend his money."

Whatever caused the impulse, Mario had it for the rest of his life. The thing that most men fought for, he fought to get rid of.

One night when Mario slept at George's home, George tried to question him about it, but Mario brushed the queries aside.

"It's only money," he'd say. "Let's talk about the opera."

They stretched out on a big double bed and started to make up names for imaginary opera stars.

"When I suggested that 'Apollo Apollo' might be a great name, and that maybe one of us should adopt it, Mario broke up," says George. "His fat stomach rumbled and rolled with laughter. Not another moment was spent on the subject of money."

In late January, 1945, the Army, finding that Mario was in "poor" health, presumably from his postnasal drip and an ear infection, granted him a medical discharge at McCaw General Hospital in Walla Walla, Washington.

6. A New Beginning

$\mathcal{L}$IKE many ex-GIs who have survived the battles, boredom and bedlam of their Army years, Mario was convinced no woman would be landing him for quite a while. He told George London repeatedly that Betty Hicks was the dangerous one. "She's trying to hook me, but she hasn't a chance. I'm not the marrying kind."

"I think Betty will get you," George would say.

"Are you kidding?"

On April 13, 1945, Mario and Betty were married by a minister in Hollywood. Then, in July, they were married by a priest in New York.

They settled down to live in New York, in the modest apartment on 49th Street. But there was nothing modest about the way the couple lived. Mario became a specialist in spending all the money he made, and money he wasn't making, too. If he was broke most of the time it wasn't because he wasn't working. He had occasional concert dates, and he had some fairly lucrative radio assignments, substituting for Jan Peerce on the Celanese radio program, *Great Moments in Music*, at a fee of $500 per appearance. Considering how short he was on formal training at this time, this was fantastic progress.

But substantial progress was also being made in the direction of total bankruptcy. Betty, proud of the accomplishments of the benedict in her house, was unwilling or incapable of exercising a strong, moderating influence on Mario. In fact, she was afflicted by many of the same temptations. She was pretty, sweet, and lacking in the maturity and understanding that a wild, unrestrained, somewhat vulgar young man like Mario needed as a support. Betty could not help him in the early years, and later, when he became completely unmanageable, she was too confused and bitter to help herself.

It was while Mario was floundering financially and searching aimlessly for some prop in his career that Sam Weiler entered his life.

Weiler, a small, dark-haired, mustached man with a secret yen to make a mark in the music world, had a lyric tenor voice that was being coaxed along at $5 an hour by Polly Robinson, a singing teacher in the Carnegie Hall Building in New York. He also had a substantial income as a realtor: he was in the business of selling and refinancing buildings with his brother Jack Weiler, who for years had been active in the Federation of Jewish Philanthropies of New

York. Along with Ben Swig, Sam and Jack operated the Fairmont and St. Francis hotels in San Francisco.

But Sam would have given up all of these worldly goods for recognition as a singer. Miss Robinson, who felt he had a pleasant enough voice, one day asked Sam if he would like to listen to a "really great voice." Sam Weiler suspected that this was Polly's polite way of informing him that his own potential was rather limited, but he was willing to listen.

The next time Sam came by for a lesson, Polly produced her star pupil. Sam sat quietly in a corner of the studio room as Mario Lanza launched into his private audition. When the performance was over, Sam Weiler knew that his own career was at an end, that he would have to live vicariously through the voice of this young man in front of him.

"What's the sense in my continuing to take lessons?" Sam said to Polly. "I couldn't sing like that in a million years."

As of that day, Sam Weiler stopped singing.

"I knew then and there," Sam says, "that I had just heard the greatest voice in the world."

As soon as Mario's lesson was over, Sam went downstairs with him to a coffee shop. Betty joined them. The three lingered for several hours over their coffee—"We had 15 cups," remembers Sam—and Mario told Sam about his inability to save his money, his debts to clothing stores and hotels and fine restaurants. He spoke to Sam about his voice and confided that if he only knew what to do with it, how to train it, he would undoubtedly become the next Enrico Caruso.

After what Sam had heard in the studio, he needed no persuasion. It was just a question of what should be done first.

Sam went immediately to Conductor Peter Herman Adler, the musical director of NBC's televised operas.

"I want to know what you think of Mario Lanza," said Weiler.

Adler had been trying to work with Mario. The job had been given him by Arthur Judson, the head of Columbia Artists Management, who told him, "I'd like to see what you can do with him. He's been untamable. He'll either be the greatest tenor in the world or a singing waiter."

"I think this boy has the greatest inherent, instinctive musicality I've ever seen," said Adler to Sam Weiler. "He's not only a great singing prospect, but he has usually behaved wonderfully with me."

When Weiler asked Adler what the next step should be, provided money could be found for Mario's musical development, Adler suggested that Mario be sent at once to Maestro Enrico Rosati, a venerable voice teacher of the old school, who had trained Beniamino Gigli, generally considered the successor to Caruso, and others like Giacomo Lauri-Volpi.

Several days later Sam brought Mario to Rosati's studio on West 57th Street. The white-haired, seventy-two-year-old instructor glared at the prospect sitting in his musty, high-ceilinged room choked with pictures of opera immortals and well-thumbed books about music.

Respectfully and fearfully Mario sang a song for him, then waited next to the grand piano as Sam left the room to talk to the maestro.

"Are you at all impressed with this boy?" Sam asked.

Rosati, his nearsighted eyes magnified behind his glasses, looked for a long moment at Sam. Then he said: "If he could make love to an old woman with money, it would be in a good cause, for she would give him the money for lessons."

"That won't be necessary, Maestro," said Weiler. "I'll be the old woman. I am ready to invest my money in this boy. I simply want to know your honest opinion of the voice.

"My friend," answered Rosati, with a little laugh, "if he fails miserably he can always be a great success singing in one of your hotels."

"I want you to teach him," said Sam.

Early in 1946, Weiler and Mario made an agreement. Sam would give Mario and Betty $70 a week to live on; he would provide Mario with clothes and Mario's folks with a small allowance. He would pay for vacations; he would pay off Mario's debts, which ran over $10,000; and he would pay $130 a month for Mario's 13 one-hour lessons with Rosati. In return for this Weiler would receive 10 percent of Mario's future gross earnings.

The hard-shelled businessman had become a patron of the arts, as well as something of a second father to this boy. And his sound business instinct held the same position on Lanza as his sentiments: he was utterly convinced of the boy's destiny.

The 15 months with Maestro Rosati were hectic, difficult, and often frustrating for Mario. They were doubly so for the maestro, for he had conceived of this boy as his greatest protégé since Gigli. "I have waited thirty-four years for you," he said. "You have a voice blessed by God!"

But if the voice was blessed by God, the temperament and discipline and attitude weren't. There were the times when the maestro was forced to listen to Mario's excuses for not preparing his lessons. "I left my books in the subway," Mario would tell Rosati. Or he'd insist, "My wife has the key to the apartment, and I couldn't get in to get my books."

"No books, no lessons," the maestro would inform him sternly.

The maestro would curse, yell, fume, exhort. *"Porco miserio!"* he'd shout. *"Stupido!"*

Then a magnificent sound would fill the room and he would suddenly be pleased. His rage would dwindle, and the boy would feel welcome again.

"To carve a work of art," Rosati says today, recapturing those months with a man who might have been his eternal monument to opera, "you must have the tools and the proper piece of wood. In Mario I had the proper piece of wood. But he was rushed, rushed."

The *"bocca grande"* of Mario was not enough for Rosati. He wanted a polished, finished singer—an artist who had learned his *solfeggio* (sight singing using solfa syllables), his theory, and perhaps an instrument to give him a more complete background. It is true that many top singers today never learned *solfeggio*. I know many who don't and won't learn it. But learning to read and write music is something that takes will power, discipline, and training—and these three things Mario had never exhibited to any degree.

He wasn't drinking in those days and he was usually on time for his lessons. But all the haranguing and all the pleading from Rosati did not supply him with the discipline he lacked. Nor were they able to purge Mario of the fears and tensions he felt, and continually lived with, beneath his cockiness and grandiloquent gestures.

In those months Mario, knowing secretly of his inadequacies as an artist, failed Rosati. And the old teacher became convinced that the boy was "afraid." There is nothing wrong, of course, in artists—even great ones—being afraid. I know many who have always competed with their private agonies and fears, yet have delivered when the time came. Caruso himself would nervously smoke cigarettes in the wings before going on. But it was these fears, accentuated and multiplied as time went on, that wore out Mario. His blustering temperament masked his perennial state of panic. I don't think he ever really got over this feeling.

For weeks Rosati had pointed Mario for an audition before the incomparable Arturo Toscanini. Intensive preparation on Verdi's "Requiem" was given to Mario.

On the day of the audition, the phone rang in Rosati's studio. The maestro was called to the phone by his woman assistant.

"What do you want?" asked Rosati.

"I can't come to the audition today, Maestro Rosati," said Mario. "I am sick. I can't sing."

"You are not sick, boy. You are afraid," said the teacher. "You must get over this. You *must* sing."

Rosati knew there were those who wanted to rush Mario in his career. He resented this desperate hurry. And now even he was rushing him. Mario knew instinctively he wasn't prepared to sing for Toscanini. In later years he told me so repeatedly: "They were rushing me, Costa. Everybody was rushing me and I couldn't go any faster. I wasn't ready."

The maestro was disappointed. But still he would not give up on the boy. Mario needed more time, more long hours of study. Maybe the *solfeggio*, the theory, could be pounded into his head in spite of himself. He would keep trying, for this was a voice with timbre, color, beauty and range. This was the voice that had been brought to him for his guidance. He must be patient with him. He must also try to keep others from pushing him before he was ready.

Today, Rosati remembers when a group interested in speeding Mario's career assembled in his studio.

"I looked at them sitting there, and I told them," says Rosati, "that I wanted to wring their necks. 'You have the goose that can lay the golden eggs and you want to kill him.' "

Rosati felt that the boy was being sacrificed on an altar of money. But then, as a perfectionist, he had to feel that way. It may have been that Mario's capacity for learning was limited to what he had already absorbed, that additional years with Rosati would have yielded little more than increased frustration. Whatever the truth, Mario venerated his irascible teacher.

Today a picture of the slim, handsome Mario of 1946 sits on top of a bookcase in Maestro Rosati's living room. There is an inscription across the bottom of the photograph:

> *To MAESTRO ENRICO ROSATI—any success I am having or will have in the future I owe 100% to you, the greatest undisputed voice teacher in the world, past, present and future. I love you and you will always be close to me wherever I am or in whatever I do. Especially on the stage however, you will always be there with the third register. All of my love for you, Maestro.*
>
> MARIO LANZA

7. With the Bel Canto Trio

WHILE Enrico Rosati was trying to mold young Mario with his own store of musical wisdom, another pupil, George London, also sought instruction from him.

In recent years London, who named himself after Jack London because he was partial to his adventurous novels, has become a distinguished member of the Metropolitan Opera. But in those days he was a high-spirited bass baritone, with possibly half the promise of a Mario Lanza. However, he Worked assiduously with Rosati, learned his trade, and grew continually as the years went by.

Out of loyalty to the old buddy of his Anny days in California, Mario helped George obtain an important assignment with him and a blond soprano named Frances Yeend. Columbia Artists was eager to have Mario and Frances as two-thirds of a *bel canto* trio that would tour the United States, Canada, Newfoundland and Mexico on an operatic odyssey. When Columbia started its search for a third singer, Mario stopped them abruptly.

"Let's take George London," he insisted.

So George joined Mario and Frances, who had already appeared together in St. Louis and at Grant Park, in Chicago, in 1948.

For two seasons, from July 8, 1947, when the three appeared in Milwaukee, until May 27, 1948, when they sang their valedictory in Moncton, New Brunswick, they won the hearts of their audiences. They sang in Ames, Iowa; Minot, North Dakota; Chihuahua, Mexico; La Porte, Indiana; Albion, Michigan; Middletown, New York; Sylacauga, Alabama; and Wallingford, Connecticut. They also appeared in St. Paul, Minnesota; Chicago; San Antonio, Texas; Madison, Wisconsin; Wheeling, West Virginia; and Halifax, Nova Scotia. They sang everywhere.

The reviewers and music critics were profoundly impressed with all three of these attractive young artists. But it was Mario who invariably caught the biggest bouquets and never more obviously than in Chicago, where on two successive nights in July, 1947—despite the fact it rained one of the evenings—the Bel Canto Trio attracted over 120,000 people into Grant Park. Claudia Cassidy, writing in the Chicago *Sunday Tribune*, completely lost her heart to Mario:

> A coltish youngster with the wide shoulders and the general just-out-of-uniform air of *Call Me Mister*, Mr. Lanza sings for the indisputable reason that he was born to sing. He has a superbly natural tenor, which he uses by instinct, and though a

multitude of fine points evade him, he possesses the things almost impossible to learn. He knows the accent that makes a lyric line reach the audience, and he knows why opera is music drama . . . a completely dramatic aria of "Celeste Aida" . . . was beautifully done, and the crowd roared while Mr. Lanza happily mopped his brow. He seemed more surprised and just as delighted as anyone else.

Mr. Lanza's solos were sung with "animation" and "imagination," said another Chicago critic.

After the trio sang in Ames, Iowa, at Iowa State College, Tolbert MacRae, head of the college's department of music, said: "Lanza gave me as great a thrill as I have had for a long time in listening to a singer."

In Milwaukee, on the night of July 8, 1947, Mario led the Bel Canto Trio before over 6,000 people, in a "Music Under The Stars" concert at the Emil Blatz Temple of Music. When it was over, Edward P. Halline of the Milwaukee *Sentinel* wrote that he had just seen "three young American singers definitely on the way up . . . Lanza was the most impressive of all, with just the kind of a voice that is needed to get all the drama out of such emotionally charged arias as "E lucevan le stelle" and "Celeste Aida." The audience roared its appreciation, vainly demanding an encore.

A few weeks later, when the Bel Canto Trio appeared in Wheeling, West Virginia's Oglebay Park Amphitheatre, Marjorie Toatgio of the Wheeling *Intelligencer*, stated that "dark-eyed Mario Lanza sang with deep feeling, a warm, appealing, tender tone, that produced an ovation with his first solo selections . . ."

Richard S. Davis of the Milwaukee *Journal* wrote on July 9, 1947, that "the favorite with the audience was the tenor, Lanza, a singer unmistakably destined to enjoy a handsome career . . . this

THE MARIO LANZA STORY

youngster not only has a firm and ringing voice of adequate power, but he has set up standards for himself and is eager to meet them. Clearly he is on his way. . ."

However, away from the concert stage and out of sight of the captious, discerning stares of the music page journalists, Mario and George were having themselves a rollicking time.

"We overate, overdrank, overslept, overdid things generally," London said of this tour. Miss Yeend, the headliner on the tour, receiving 45 percent, or approximately $500 for each concert, to Mario's 30 percent and London's 25 percent, was forced to put up with their peccadilloes.

"I was a house mother and watchdog for both of them," says Miss Yeend, who came out of Vancouver, Washington, to embark on a singing career. "I had heard Mario was a heavy drinker, and there were times when he did his share of drinking on that tour. But we tried to make a pact in each city we visited that we wouldn't drink. He kept to it pretty well. It wasn't the drinking so much as the pranks that almost drove me out of my mind."

Even in those days, singing for good money, Mario was up to his old boyhood trick of loading his pockets with food, candy, and delicacies and walking out of stores without paying.

Sometimes he would amble into a record shop, walk to the counter and nonchalantly break off the edges of discs by performers who did not appeal to him. To the best of my knowledge, he was never caught in the act, but to this day certain record store proprietors must be convinced that their merchandise was the target of mice.

Throughout the Bel Canto tour Mario lived in accordance with the pattern he had established when Sam Weiler first encountered him. Invariably he chose the best, most expensive hotel in town, then ensconced himself in the best, most expensive suite, where he had the best, most expensive food sent up to him. He also distributed the best tips most of the townspeople had ever seen.

Occasionally when he felt especially lonely or depressed, Betty would join him. But his companionship with George usually was enough to sustain him as the trio wended its way from one town to another.

Since Mario had always feared planes, he simply refused to travel in them. This meant that he was always traveling by bus or train with George, while Frances Yeend would go on alone by plane. It also put the burden of advance arrangements on Frances' shoulders, and made tight schedules for the trio's rear guard.

Once, when George and Mario slept late, they missed a through bus to Mexico City. Forced to ship out on a local bus, of sorts, which was scheduled to make a long series of stops in small towns, they had to share their space with livestock, mothers and babies along the way.

The heat became so intense, and their throats so dry, that the two tarrying singers started drinking wine. The wine led to extemporaneous song. Everyone on the caravan seemed to forget the dirt and the muggy weather as Mario and George gave out with their full repertoire. As each song ended, the passengers applauded mightily. These people, mostly poor Mexicans, had never been so thrilled in their lives.

When the bus finally arrived in Mexico City, Mario and George were not only logy with wine but also so hoarse they couldn't sing another note. Frances, having pulled into town well ahead of them, could do little more than waggle a tapering finger in their bloodshot eyes.

Despite these shenanigans, the months with the Bel Canto Trio could well have been the most serious period of Mario's musical career. Prior to joining the trio, he had given two performances in New Orleans of *Madama Butterfly*, the first occasion—since Tanglewood that he had sung in opera, and the last time he was ever to do so. This, followed by the rigorous Bel Canto tour, represented his most diligent effort.

"He studied seriously with the Bel Canto Trio," recalls George London. "He was a sincere enthusiast of all things vocal. We used to have passionate discussions until all hours of the night about the relative merits of the masters. He had an uncanny knack for recognizing voices and imitating them."

Though Mario's behavior was the despair of Frances Yeend, London still feels that these were Mario's "best disciplined months."

With a touch of wistfulness, London adds: "If he could only have crawled out of his own skin and listened to his own voice, he might have lived his whole life differently."

Mario was so intensely interested in his art in those days that he would travel miles to hear a record. When he learned that a Philadelphia restaurant had a rare record by an obscure Italian singer named Alessandro Valente, Mario made sure to visit the place with George, even though his hometown was not on the tour's regular schedule.

He also continued to show concern for what his folks would think of him. Frances Yeend recalls the day he showed her $200 in one-dollar bills. "I'm going to count it out for my parents, then I'm going to give it all to them," Mario said. "They'll be proud of me."

While Mario was conquering the country with his two co-performers, RCA Victor was making test records of his voice, in anticipation of the moment when he would be ready to record commercially.

Somehow, these records found their way to Ida Koverman, valued amanuensis of Louis B. Mayer, still the all-powerful chief at Metro-Goldwyn-Mayer. The Russian-born tycoon who had made decisions affecting the lives of Greta Garbo, Greer Garson and Clark Gable, now was about to make one affecting the future of a boy from South Philadelphia named Mario Lanza.

Mayer, excited by the records played for him by Miss Koverman, wanted to hear more. Ida, used to association with the mighty (having served as secretary to Herbert Hoover before he became President) and also used to giving orders and having them followed out, exercised her persuasive powers on the officials of the Hollywood Bowl.

A date was set—August 28, 1947—for Mario to interrupt his tour and appear in the Hollywood Bowl. Frances Yeend would appear with him. And George London would be in the audience.

Frances, who had been hospitalized in New York briefly, flew out to Hollywood to join Mario for the concert. When she met Mario, he flashed a sign of annoyance. He seemed disappointed that she had actually come. He sensed he was there to be tested, exhibited. He knew this was the moment that might make him or break him, as far as Hollywood was concerned.

He wanted the stage to himself that night.

He was to get it.

8. Open, Sesame

*J*UST like the old girl in "La donna è mobile," one of Mario's favorite arias, Hollywood has earned the reputation of being fickle. It will love, worship and adore; it will then reject and ignore in short order.

But when Mario appeared under the stars that August night in 1947, he had a squadron of claquers on hand from his *Winged Victory* days. They came to cheer him on to fame in the velvety darkness of the California night. What they lacked in numbers (attendance was only 3,896 in the Hollywood Bowl that evening—less than the season's average) they made up for in noise and enthusiasm. Dozens of celebrities had come to hear Mario. So had Ida Koverman, Louis B. Mayer, Eddie O'Brien, and George London.

With Eugene Ormandy conducting, Mario sang two arias—Donizetti's "Una furtiva lagrima" from the opera *L'Elisir d'Amore*; Giordano's "Un di, all' azzuro spazio" from the opera *Andrea Chénier*. Then, teaming with his long-suffering road companion, Frances Yeend, he rendered two duets: Verdi's "Parigi, o cara" from *La Traviata* and Puccin's "O! Quant' occhi fisi" from *Madama Butterfly*.

Bravely camouflaging the fear and uncertainty that gripped him, Mario even introduced one of his numbers, stumbling slightly in the process. The *faux pas* drew a roar from the crowd—a roar of sympathy and support. Mario knew then that he was ahead of the game.

"He sang that night as he never sang before or after," insists George London.

A great vote of approval swept Hollywood after the concert, and a barrage of offers came Mario's way. But it remained for Louis B. Mayer, in the last stage of his kingpin role at M-G-M, to be the architect of the plan that would bring Mario Lanza to Metro. Mayer was never a man to underplay or understate. He went in for vulgar display, for the mawkish, for melodramatic histrionics. But in his more than three decades as a surly, controversial despot, he had demonstrated a fantastic ability to pick winners. And now he was ready to anoint Mario with his peculiar blessing.

Within 72 hours of Mario's appearance at the Hollywood Bowl, Mayer sent out an urgent call to his producers, directors, and top executives to meet on the mammoth M-G-M recording stage known to all as Stage One.

Among those who came, none of them suspecting what was to transpire, was producer Joe Pasternak, the man who discovered Deanna Durbin, a little girl once second only to Shirley Temple in the affections of movie-goers. Pasternak had also been instrumental in enticing such prominent classical music figures as Lauritz Melchior, José Iturbi and Leopold Stokowski into the film factories.

Miss Koverman had wanted Pasternak to see Mario in his appearance at the Hollywood Bowl. But Mrs. Pasternak was on the verge of giving birth to a son, so Pasternak couldn't make it. Now Mayer was going to bring Lanza to him.

When everyone had assembled on Stage One, the big speakers were moved in. Then, as L. B. gave an imperious hand signal, a tremendous voice echoed throughout the cavernous recording area.

"It was a thundering voice," says Pasternak. "It was rich, warm and virile and mounted to incredible highs. It made my spine tingle and the room shake."

Pasternak whispered to one of the factotums standing next to him. "It's like Caruso himself coming back to life," he said in awe.

After the voice boomed out two more songs, Mayer motioned that the strange and unexpected audition was at an end. When the applause, crashing and positive in its approbation, broke out, it was something more than mere "yes man" affirmation of the Boss's wishes.

"Now," said Mayer after a moment of suspense, "I'd like you to meet the man who is the owner of this God-given voice."

Mario, grinning and flushed, walked on stage. His dark eyes flickered over the sea of executive faces.

"He looked like a trained tiger," recalls Pasternak. "His hair was bushy and he looked squat and mussed. But there was something attractive about him."

Mayer turned to Mario and, with a paternalistic nod, thanked him for coming to the M-G-M studio. Then Mayer waited for Mario to depart.

"I wanted you to hear this man," he said, "because we have decided to sign him to a contract. Any producer who is interested, come and speak to me."

The drama on Stage One, made to order by Louis B. Mayer, had come to an end. It then remained for Joe Pasternak to seek out his chief and tell him of his desire to work with Mario Lanza, as he had worked with so many other stars of opera, operetta and the concert stage.

It happened precisely that way. Pasternak, a keen judge of musical talent and box-office appeal, approached Mayer. He had been impressed with Mario's virility, his strength, his tremendous voice. And he also judged Mario would survive the lens, with its capacity to distort and caricature.

"I think I like this boy," said Pasternak to the beaming Mayer. "I'd like to make a picture with him."

"I'm grateful to you," said Mayer.

Later in the day Pasternak, seeking a quick study on his new disciple, lunched with Mario at the M-G-M commissary. Mario was respectful in his manner. He told Pasternak that he knew of his achievements with others, like Deanna Durbin. Even if Pasternak was used to this approach from his protégés, he was genuinely impressed with what seemed to be Mario's quality of ingenuousness.

Though Pasternak was later to be the butt of many of Mario's unpredictable tantrums, there were few surface signs then of Mario's instability or emotional troubles. He could be almost saintly when he wanted to—and that day his graciousness toward Pasternak was sincere and heartfelt. It was to make Mario's future behavior upsetting and eternally puzzling to Pasternak.

A few days after Mario's first lunch with Pasternak, he was invited to Pasternak's home with Betty. While talking to Joe's wife, Mario leaned on a priceless glass table in Pasternak's garden. The table smashed into several small pieces. Mario was visibly upset by the incident, and didn't quite know how to apologize.

"That's all right, Mario," said Pasternak. "It's a good omen."

It was quite the opposite.

9. *"That Midnight Kiss"*

*I*N THE hectic hours before Mario signed on the dotted line for Louis B. Mayer, big-money offers were coming in from all sides. In desperation he phoned Sam Weiler in New York. "Sam," he pleaded, "I've got to do something right away. Everyone's after me! What do you want me to sign?"

"Don't sign anything," yelled Sam. "I'll be out there the first thing in the morning!"

Sam did get there in the morning, and the M-G-M contract he approved was a good one.

Mario was given a $10,000 bonus to sign a seven-year contract, at a starting salary of $750 a week for 20 weeks. He was to work for M-G-M six months a year. The rest of the time would be his own, to sing concerts, study, pursue an operatic career—do anything he desired. He would receive $15,000 for his first picture and $25,000 for the second. Ultimately, he was to make $75,000 per film.

At the same time that Sam closed the contract with M-G-M, a new agreement was drawn up between Mario and Sam, with Sam consenting to serve as personal manager and agent in return for 20 percent of Mario's gross earnings.

When Mario's contract with M-G-M was ready for signing, Mayer himself showed up for the festivities.

"Mario, my boy," said Mayer, in his avuncular manner, "I'm going to make you a singing Clark Gable."

Pasternak grinned his approval. "This is the first time," he said, "I'll be able to let an operatic tenor sing and know the audience out front isn't closing its eyes and visualizing Van Johnson." It never occurred to Joe that Mario at 170 pounds was almost 100 pounds under his top weight.

Now that he was working for M-G-M, Mario was quite eager to earn his money. He wanted to know all the parts Joe Pasternak had in mind for him to do, and what he should do to prepare for them.

But first came the screen test. For a few frightening hours it almost succeeded in throwing all of Pasternak's plans out of joint.

When Mario arrived for his color test with Kathryn Grayson, his hair looked wild and the suit he was wearing emphasized his width, rather than his height. "He ran to loose-fitting shirts, with long-stemmed collars," says Pasternak, "and this was the poorest possible way to show off his charm."

When the results of the test were shown, some of the second-guessers on the M-G-M lot sneered that L. B. had really pulled a "rock." Pasternak, himself distraught, wasted little time mourning the failure of the test or trying to rebut the critics.

He called Mario to his office. He studied Mario's hair—"It looked like a horsehair mattress that had burst its seams"—then the big chest and the fresh, almost seraph-like face.

"You'll do," Joe said, "but we'll have to make some changes."

Mario was sent immediately to the hairdresser, where his hair was dyed reddish-black and carefully parted on one side.

When he returned to Pasternak's office, his hair looked manageable and less wiry, and there was a new, soft quality about his face that had been lacking in the disastrous screen test.

"We'll have to give you another test right away," said Pasternak, delighted with the subtle changes in his charge.

When the second screen test was exhibited, some of those who had scoffed at the first scarcely recognized Lanza.

It now remained for Pasternak to choose Mario's first movie for M-G-M. "I thought it might be a good idea," says Pasternak, "to do practically a take-off on Mario's own life."

Writers were called in, and though Mario's real life, if it had been followed honestly and authentically, encompassed all of the drama necessary to provide an excellent screen theme, changes were made and fiction added. The popular legend that Mario had been a piano mover or a truck driver in Philadelphia probably emanated from this first movie, which was called *That Midnight Kiss*.

Pasternak surrounded Mario with acting veterans like Ethel Barrymore, who played the part of a wealthy Philadelphia matron trying to organize an opera company for the sake of a granddaughter (Kathryn Grayson) with musical aspirations. Keenan Wynn, J. Carrol Naish, Jules Munshin, and José Iturbi, who played the role of a symphony conductor, were also in the cast. Norman Taurog was the director, and Charles Previn, who had known one of Mario's uncles from the old Roxy Theater days in New York, was the musical director. Uncle Jules Cocozza had once been a contractor for the Roxy.

Both Taurog and Previn found Mario extremely cooperative and willing. Knowing of Mario's incredible appetite, Taurog insisted that a scale be kept in Mario's dressing room, so that he could weigh in each morning when he arrived for work, much like a prizefighter in training.

And Mario was in training. It was in a Hollywood gym that he met Terry Robinson, a muscular, slim-waisted physical culture enthusiast who had been a welterweight boxing champion with the United States Army in 1942. Terry became Mario's best and most steadfast friend.

There was an occasional admonition from Previn to "save some of those high notes," but Mario never got out of hand, never rebelled, never was insulting.

"I told him," says Previn, who is a psychologist today, "that he was going to be a big success, that he shouldn't let it go to his head."

But if all seemed serene on the surface there were signs that Mario hadn't lost any of his boyhood fears and anxieties.

"We finished the picture and it was a pleasant enough experience," says Pasternak, "but there was a disturbing quality, even then, that you couldn't quite pin down."

Part of this quality was boastfulness, by which Mario covered his insecurity. "I'm greater than Caruso," he told Joe one day on the set of *That Midnight Kiss.*

"You might become as great, or even greater," Pasternak said carefully, "but you've got a long way to go."

And already Pasternak had begun to have difficulty gauging the moods of Mario. "One day he was at my feet, the next day at my throat," he says. The humility Joe had observed on their first meetings showed less and less; more and more Mario was the first-person chest pounder.

Now began a new and dangerous strain in Mario's behavior—a vicious hostility bordering on paranoia. When Edmond O'Brien, pleased with Mario's quick rise to eminence, came to visit him during the filming of *That Midnight Kiss*, Mario was overjoyed to see him but gave him no chance to relive the rowdy, ribald memories they shared. Mario was interested only in telling O'Brien of the dark, sinister things people were trying to do to him.

"That old bitch Ethel Barrymore," Mario hissed, "she's trying to steal my scenes. I'll tell her where to get off!"

Eddie was fascinated. The idea of a Barrymore trying to take advantage of a novice was ludicrous.

"She never does anything like that, Mario," Eddie said. "Ethel's one of the—"

Mario interrupted with a savage curse.

"She's no damn good, she's upstaging me all the time! Who the hell does she think she is?" And as he raved on about Ethel Barrymore, Mario's eyes, ordinarily so bright, narrowed into searing pinpoints of hate. O'Brien was powerless to stop the tirade.

"Maybe I should have recognized it at once," O'Brien says, "but who looks for paranoia in a friend? Mario suddenly believed that he was being persecuted, that almost everyone was insidiously working against him. To most of us at the time, Mario was only a youngster with a wonderful, thrilling voice. We thought we could kid him and make jokes about him without having him hate us. Lord, that hatred must have been burning inside him all along!"

I thought I too detected this hostility in Mario. Later I became intimately acquainted with it on our concert trips around the country. The generous, affectionate side of Mario, his boundless warmth for ordinary people, his love and loyalty for his friends, made it impossible to regard him as a sick man. The ugly side of Mario was overlooked until darker days, when it was too late to give him the help he needed so badly.

That Midnight Kiss, produced for approximately one million dollars by M-G-M, was such a great financial success that M-G-M paid Mario $25,000 for the movie, $10,000 more than his contract called for.

Among the songs Mario sang in the movie were Jerome Kern's "They Didn't Believe Me"; "Celeste Aïda"; "Una furtiva lagrima"; "I Know, I Know, I Know"; and "Love Is Music," based on Tchaikovsky's Fifth Symphony and adapted by Charles Previn, with lyrics by William Katz.

Though the reviewers were not unqualified in their praise of Mario, M-G-M's moguls couldn't help but be pleased—even when Harold Barnes of the New York *Herald Tribune* said: "He may have a resounding tenor voice, but he has a lot to learn about acting."

Bosley Crowther, the *New York Times* critic, let José Iturbi carry his message. Iturbi said: "His voice has quality and warmth. And he has a nice personality."

But it remained for *Variety* to accurately predict great things for Mario:

> The film introduces a potentially smash b.o. draw in tenor Mario Lanza. His standout singing and capable thesping should provide an extra word-of-mouth fillip for exhibitors. His voice, when he's singing opera, is excellent. In addition, far from resembling the caricatured opera tenor, he's a nice-looking youngster of the average American boy school, who will have the femme customers on his side from the start . . .

This, of course, is precisely what happened. When *That Midnight Kiss* was sneak-previewed in the Picwood Theater in Westwood, where Mario always went for his previews, the Lanza rendition of "Celeste Aida" threw the bobby-soxers into pandemonium. To the satraps and seers at M-G-M, this could mean only one thing: a new celebrity had just been born.

10. On Tour Again

$\mathcal{S}$INCE his childhood, it appeared, Mario had been living a split emotional life, with periods of extreme exhilaration and black depression following in cycle. Now, with the start of a Hollywood career, his professional life was split, too. Six months a year he would devote to M-G-M and his movies, the other six months to his concerts and—we all hoped—serious operatic study.

Before *The Midnight Kiss* was released, Mario and I embarked on our first cross-country concert tour. It was just two years from the time we had worked on our first concert at Shippensburg, Pennsylvania. This concert business was now a considerably different matter for Mario. At Shippensburg he had been a relative unknown, engaged in a fierce struggle for recognition. Now he had more than emerged from obscurity; he was a man on the verge of great stardom, a figure precariously balanced on the brink of overnight fame.

Columbia Artists had booked 27 dates for us on this tour—from Bluefield, West Virginia, on March 7, 1949, to Lincoln, Nebraska, on May 25, 1949. In between we were to pay our respects to Clinton, Iowa; Zanesville, Ohio; Athens, Ohio; Wilmington, Delaware; Troy, New York; Portland, Maine; Fort Wayne, Indiana; Duluth, Minnesota; Chicago; Minneapolis; New Orleans; Tulsa, Oklahoma; Sylacauga, Alabama; Centralia, Illinois, and Charleston, Illinois.

We opened with a cancellation in Bluefield, and closed with a cancellation in Lincoln. Out of the 27 dates, Mario was on hand for 12. He ducked out on some dates without giving a reason. For others he pleaded a cold—"pneumonia" he insisted on calling it. Sensing his imminent rise as a screen personality, and all too aware that tickets for this tour had been sold a year before, when nobody could have heard of him, Mario was as disturbed as a petulant child at the prospect of playing the "tank" towns for so little money. Already he had notions about singing in the big cities for top fees. Mario had a case of swollen pride well in advance of success.

Yet behind his cockiness there were always the lurking fears and tensions. Even for the thoroughly schooled artist, and Mario was hardly one, the concert stage is a continual challenge. Each new experience conjures up dreadful visions of forgotten lines or sour notes or sudden laughter. To Mario more than most those hours on the concert stage, facing audiences, were emotional and physical torture. He was lazy, irresponsible, and lacking a proper sense of the importance of the tour to his development as an artist, but he was also in a state of continuous fright, just as he had been at the prospect of singing for Toscanini.

Sometimes there was no accounting for his behavior. One morning he woke up complaining of a pain in his side. Immediately he phoned the local concert manager.

"I have a pain, a terrible pain," Mario said. "It's so bad I can hardly talk."

He talked surprisingly well the rest of the day—and far into the night. This in itself was unusual, for Mario, in addition to his fear of the stage, was always careful not to overuse his voice.

On May 19 we had a concert set for Centralia, Illinois. Mario seemed quite eager to sing there, for he remembered the mine disaster that had taken over 100 lives there just two years before. But when I arrived at Centralia, the president of the community's concert association told me the concert had been canceled. Mr. Lanza, he said, was quite ill in a Chicago hospital.

A few minutes later I received a call from Chicago. "What in hell are you doing in that town?" boomed Mario's healthy-sounding voice. "Why aren't you here with me?"

There had already been nine cancellations on the tour, so the fact that Mario had walked out on a $1,200 engagement did not plunge me into a state of shock. However, I tried to remind him of his obligation. As I spoke, I could hear a commotion in the background, people shouting and laughing.

"What's going on there?" I demanded.

"Costa, I've got some wonderful friends here," roared Mario. "You should see what we've got to eat! You'd go crazy, Costa. They have that black caviar you're so crazy about. You better hurry up and get here, you don't want to miss it!"

"I thought you were in the hospital," I said dully. "Are you all right?"

"What hospital? Are you kidding?"

"Mario, you come down here and sing."

"No, you get here quick, the Bismarck Hotel, before the food runs out." For a moment there was a pause. Then Mario continued: "Anyway, I don't know some of those numbers they put on the program. Those Hugo Wolf songs I don't know from nothing."

Understanding then why Mario wasn't going to keep the date, I caught the next train to Chicago, arrived at 9 P.M., and checked in at the Bismarck. When I walked into Mario's room the party was still in full swing. Two tables were loaded down with food and wines and liquor. A voice teacher, Mario Sciapio, was there, and several other friends. If Mario was embarrassed by his failure to make the Centralia concert, he didn't show a sign of it—at first.

But later in the evening he put his arm around me. I had the feeling he was trying to tell me something important. But he didn't. Instead, he reached for the "big promise," his favorite device for avoiding unpleasant realities.

"Costa," he said, expansively, "I'm going to have you conduct for me when I do my RCA Victor records."

That night, exhilarated by the surroundings, the wine, the food, the people, Mario sang until four in the morning. I couldn't help but think of those disappointed people in Centralia, who would have listened eagerly to this extemporaneous performance.

I was sure that if Mario had his way, he would have invited all of them up to the room to hear him—for nothing.

On March 25, Mario did keep his appointment with the people of Zanesville. He sang a typical concert:

Lamento di Federico, from *L'Arlesiana* by Francesco Cilea
Celeste Aïda, from *Aïda* by Giuseppe Verdi
Lasciatemi Morire by Claudio Monteverdi
Gia il sole dal Gange by Alessandro Scarlatti
Nina by Pergolesi

This was followed by three of my solo piano selections. Then Mario went on with:

Agnus Dei by Bizet
La donna é mobile, from *Rigoletto* by Verdi

After the intermission I spelled Mario again with three numbers. Then he concluded the program with these numbers:

The House on the Top of the Hill by Ernest Charles
My Lady Walks in Loveliness by Ernest Charles
Tell Me, O Blue, Blue Sky by Vittorio Giannini
Softly as in the Morning Sunrise by Sigmund Romberg
Thine Alone by Victor Herbert

After the concert, one of the Zanesville grande dames approached Mario. "Wonderful, Mr. Lanza, wonderful," she said. "We hope you'll come back—in the spring, to see the daffodils?"

"Why, of course," said Mario. "We'll be back."

In years to come this was a standing joke between Mario and me, but with a note of wistfulness in it. No matter where spring found us—in Rome, London, Hawaii, Hollywood, New York-

Mario would always say: "We didn't make it back to Zanesville this spring to see the daffodils, did we?"

During the tour we came through New York, and Mario had the chance to meet Nicky Brodszky for the first time. Nicky was a talented young song writer who had been brought over from Europe by Joe Pasternak to work on new songs for Mario. Pasternak felt "their styles were harmonious." It was a brilliant hunch: "Be My Love," a song Nicky wrote (lyrics by Sammy Cahn) for Mario's second picture, *Toast of New Orleans*, sold over one million copies in one year, over 1,800,000 all told, and became Mario's top all-time best seller with RCA Victor Red Seal, assuring him a ranking with such celebrated Red Seal artists as Van Cliburn, Arthur Fiedler's Boston Pops, the Robert Shaw Chorale, and Toscanini.

Nicky had been having a difficult time making ends meet in his newly adopted country. So Mario, who took an instant liking to him and called him "boychik," helped to subsidize him until the big break came. The gesture was as typical of Mario as the two-hundred-dollar watches he would present in a sudden display of affection and magnanimity.

Meanwhile, Mario's appetite was becoming more and more of a problem. I shared his great interest in food, if not his capacity for it. Many times while traveling we would hold up our gin rummy games or our three- or four-handed poker games to talk about the types of cooking we cherished. I boasted of my mother's artistry—especially with a pinkish dish named "taramosalata," the Greek national appetizer which is compounded of imported Norwegian fish roe, salted and treated discreetly with onions, bread, olive oil and lemon. Mario, warming to the subject, would counter with elaborate descriptions of what his mother Maria would concoct in her kitchen.

The first time I told Mario about taramosalata, he couldn't wait to get off the train and into the Acropolis Restaurant in Chicago. He proceeded to gulp down five double orders of the dish, which is quite salty and loaded with calories, and at once I named him president of the Taramosalata Society. It was the beginning of a great love affair between Mario and this particular delicacy. In later years I must have put on my apron and made it for the Lanza family fifty times.

It wasn't only with this Greek dish that Mario distinguished himself. His favorites were steak four inches thick (he'd always search, in each city he visited, for a good steak house, one that might have meats cured for six months), pizza, and lasagna. But he could also excel on a simple order of eggs, as he had earlier demonstrated when he had been in the cast of *Winged Victory*.

One day, when we were staying at the Hotel Pierre in New York, Mario called room service.

"Bring me," he began, "twenty fried eggs, sunny side up, with three orders of bacon and three orders of toast and three orders of sausages."

When the waiter arrived he started to set up for five people. Mario stopped him, saying, "I'm hungry this morning."

The waiter and I then looked on, goggle-eyed, as he downed eighteen of the eggs, and all of the side dishes.

When he was finished, he pushed the two leftover eggs in my direction. "Here, Costa," he said, "you eat them. I don't know what's happened to my appetite."

The routine of the concert tour became standardized after a while, and Mario and I managed to work out our own peculiar patterns.

On the trains we invariably played gin rummy, talked about food, or read magazines. Mario was never a book reader, but I have literally seen him buy out a newsstand's magazines. Our card games were played for pennies, and in those days Mario couldn't lose. "I can't help winning, Costa," Mario would say. "It's my golden touch."

I found it frustrating to lose so consistently but somehow Mario's boyish smile and great glee at winning made it worthwhile.

Around dawn (we were usually early-morning arrivals in a town) in late April we hit Minneapolis, where we had three engagements in three nights at the Apollo Club. As we trudged through the lobby of the Nicollet Hotel, practically sleepwalking, Mario noticed that the bellboys were being marched to their posts by a bell captain.

Mario, who couldn't stand the Army when he was in it, had a special hatred for signs of it in civilian life.

"Where the hell do you think you are?" he snapped at the bell captain. "Why didn't you stay in the Army if you liked it so much? Or didn't you make Pfc?"

Vaguely upset, the bell captain dismissed his marching corps and walked away.

Mario often would remain in bed till just before five in the afternoon, when he'd have a steak or a salad served in his room. Sometimes he'd slip off to a movie during the day. When we were in Duluth—for a date that Mario kept, by the way—he noticed that a local theater was already advertising the coming of his movie *That Midnight Kiss*. Mario stood outside the movie house for some time admiring the stills, then walked around the corner and bought fifty copies of a movie magazine that was running a story about him. At most of his concerts he never failed to remark about his upcoming movie. In the ingenuous way he did it, it never became an imposition on the audience.

After his five o'clock supper, Mario would start to dress for the evening performance, which generally had an 8:30 starting time. Since he despised formal dress and anything that would impede his natural movement, Mario devised an excuse. Standing in mid-stage in his regular street clothes, he would say: "I hope you'll forgive my appearance tonight, but somebody got our bags mixed up at the station, and I lost my tux."

While he dressed in the hotel, Mario would try out his voice. He'd sing the high notes and some of the phrases from his songs. When his voice was faithful, and it usually was, he was as thrilled as any bystander by its range, its feeling. Like Caruso, he had a "sob" in his voice, and a fantastic ability to give phrases extra emphasis, which was the very essence of his success as a singer. It stemmed from an intense feeling for each song. He lived what he sang.

More than once I heard Mario say, as he tested his voice, "Mario, you can sing like a son of a bitch." And there was no denying that he could.

One last tune-up and he was ready to leave for the concert hall. "We're in good voice tonight, eh Costa?" he'd say.

Downstairs, the usual reception committee would be on hand to whisk us by car to the hall. Most singers I have known want to scout the hall in which they are to sing. But Mario was hardly ever concerned about this aspect of his art. He would have sung in Ebbets Field, Carnegie Hall, Madison Square Garden, or the Los Angeles Coliseum. The physical dimensions of the plant meant absolutely nothing to him.

I always tried to avoid conversation, even small talk, in the car going to the concert hall. The reception people usually appreciated why; they had heard or read that in those few minutes before the artist was scheduled to appear, he was living in a private world, a private nightmare.

At the concert hall, in those last seconds before Mario had to meet his audience, he would remind me, with a note of grimness in his voice, that if he forgot his lines I should "throw the words" to him. "Don't let me down," he'd say. "I'm counting on you, Costa."

Mario's curtain-time insecurity was exaggerated but certainly not unique. I know of one famous singer who used to carry her lyrics in a little book hidden in a bouquet of flowers. And I have seen pianists of great reputation approach their tasks with tiny pans of warm water next to them, so that they could warm their icy cold fingers.

Once Mario appeared on stage, it was difficult to believe this was the same uncertain boy who had pleaded to be given the words. His manner was flamboyant, insouciant, like an artful prize fighter who knows how far an opponent can get with him, how many liberties he may take. There is a certain formality to the concert stage, but Mario disrupted and defied this tradition.

He wanted the audience to like him, to be awe-stricken by his talents. When he finished a number, and the applause began, he would nod, then grin broadly. It was then he knew he had the audience in the palms of his hands.

"Gee, you're wonderful," he'd tell them.

He was sweating from head to toe, for his whole body, as well as his mind and voice, were involved with his singing. Singing, opera and concert-stage variety, is a physical talent as well as an art. In many cases the singer is more athletic than intellectual. They say that when Caruso was teaching a young New York policeman, the only student he ever had, he imparted this advice: "Singing is something like defecation. But instead of straining down, you must strain up."

Invariably people caught Mario's enthusiasm in his song. His whole face would simulate the meaning of the words and phrases, helping to make the story come alive. He had an ability to project that few singers have had.

It was never necessary to remind Mario before a concert, "Give a good show tonight, Mario." When he performed, when he didn't run out because of the nameless, faceless terrors that besieged him, he never failed to give a good show. He sang as if it would be the last time on earth the song would be heard; and the fans sensed it and reacted to his feeling, his sincerity.

Afterwards the people would come backstage to see him, touch him, request an autograph. He never failed to respond to this adulation, though on this tour it was nothing compared to what would happen little more than a year later. It wasn't too far off to the black-market tickets, the stampeding at stage doors, the ripping of clothes, the hysterical screaming that once only Frank Sinatra elicited.

Mario never got tired of signing his pictures for the collectors. Back at the hotel, stripped down to his waist, he would stay up till two in the morning carefully scrawling his name and favorite message—*Wishing you the best in life always, from Mario Lanza*—on glossy photos of his boyish face.

Even today, over a year after his death, Mario's folks and Terry Robinson, the best friend he left behind, sit and mail out pictures of Mario to people all over the world, who refuse to forget his voice or his face. The requests still come in by the thousands, and none are turned down.

11. "The Toast of New Orleans"

THE golden, exuberant singing of Mario Lanza has been preserved in the many recordings made for RCA Victor. These records will keep alive the precious gift that Mario possessed long after the tales of his excesses, his fears, his anxieties have been forgotten. Then only the voice, with its expansive phrasing and its happy blend of feeling with power, will remain.

I can still remember clearly the day in May, 1949, that Mario and I joined to make our first recordings for RCA. I can recall vividly how happy Mario was that afternoon, and how, after we had completed our chores for the day, he hugged me and said, "Well, Costa, now we have done it together for posterity."

For a while it didn't seem I would conduct for Mario at any of his recording sessions. Though I had had a well-received debut as a conductor at Carnegie Hall in 1946, I had never been invited to record for a major company. I was young and relatively inexperienced; a great deal of money is involved in the business of making recordings (an expenditure of $5,000 is generally necessary to record four songs with a 55- or 60-man orchestra); and it was not surprising that RCA would have reservations about my ability to do the job competently.

However, Mario had said he wanted me to work with him. He sensed that I had faith in his natural instinct for singing and that I knew how best to guide him. He was certain that we could work successfully with an orchestra, though our previous collaboration had been one only of singer and pianist. He felt, and rightfully so, that I was truly inspired by the sound of his voice, and he had a hunch that we would be able to produce exciting and artistic results.

Originally, Mario had been offered three conductors from the Metropolitan Opera to work with. When he accepted one of them, everything seemed set. However, when they went together to the New York City Center to rehearse, it was apparent that the conductor could no more control the temperament of Mario than a complete stranger in the street. Several disagreements followed and Mario picked up his music and walked out.

The next day Mario phoned RCA and told them he wanted me to conduct for him. The company was not anxious to go along with this proposal. But since Mario seemed quite adamant about it, they were willing to make a deal. They asked Mario to guarantee the cost of the session in case we should fail to record four songs effectively in three hours.

Mario agreed, then called me and told me of my good fortune.

"I'll always be grateful to you for your kindness and your confidence in me," I said.

"Forget it, Costa," he said. "I want you with me."

The ballroom of the Manhattan Center in New York City was to be the site of our recording session. Mario phoned at ten that morning to reassure me. "This is going to be fun," he said.

With an audience limited to the orchestra, the engineers and myself, Mario seemed free of the anxieties that assailed him before concert crowds.

When I walked into the ballroom, the musicians were somewhat surprised to see such a young man. As they started to tune up, some of them looked at me in disbelief.

Mario, dressed neatly in brown sports jacket and flannel trousers, with his shirt open at the neck, stood on a little wooden platform, the microphone in front of him.

Then we started our work. Everything moved swiftly and satisfactorily. Mario was in robust voice. When he sang, however, he would close his eyes at crucial moments. This created difficulties for me: the selections we were recording had so many subtle changes of pace. However, despite my alarm at Mario's new unorthodoxy, the songs went off well. One of the selections we did that day—"Che gelida manina" from Puccini's *La Boheme*—is in the RCA Victor Hall of Fame.

After each recording, we listened intently to the playback. We knew it had gone more than satisfactorily, and the four sides were completed in substantially less time than three hours.

Mario was elated. "Costa," he laughed, "we will both be famous."

With the release of *That Midnight Kiss*, Mario was famous.

For Mario's second movie, Joe Pasternak chose *The Toast of New Orleans*, a big Technicolor musical that tried to show what life—high life, that is—was like in that colorful city at the turn of the century. Kathryn Grayson again was selected to play opposite Mario, who was cast as a poor fisherman trying to rise above his low station in life and make off with a famous opera singer.

In this film Mario hit the jackpot with Nicky Brodszky's "Be My Love," which resounded from jukeboxes, poured into homes all over the land, and became America's favorite song practically overnight. When he took over his own radio show for Coca-Cola, Mario used "Be My Love" as his theme song.

"Any remaining skepticism over Lanza's socko voice personality draw," said *Variety*, "was dissipated when his disk 'Be My Love' sold more than any single artist had ever sold for RCA-Red Seal."

On every $1.29 record of this hit that was sold, Mario received 10 percent, 5 percent more than popular singers usually receive. Red Seal's theory, which had been blown to bits by Mario's success, was that the "longhairs" were entitled to a higher percentage on each record, due to the fact that they would not sell as many records.

Mario, again under the directorial supervision of Norman Taurog, managed to control his weight during the filming of *Toast of New Orleans*, but now with the help of crash diets, pills, and shots.

Surely his rapid changes in weight, almost from one week to the next, did not have a stabilizing effect on his highly volatile personality.

Experts have often cited the hazards of excessive dieting. They point out that some overweight people become so depressed during or after a rigid diet that any improvement in their physical health and general appearance is offset by an adverse effect on their mental health.

Mario may have been a grim example of the type of dieter whose personality was twisted by continual crash programs. Kathryn Grayson felt that Mario "became impossible to work with at times during *Toast of New Orleans*," and she said, "Those shots and pills affected his personality. When I told him my opinions on the subject, we quarreled."

One day on the set, as J. Carrol Naish, who played Mario's father in the picture, waited to administer some paternal advice, his "son" failed to show up. Needless to say, this caused a stir. Taurog was still burning when late in the day he finally caught sight of Mario walking unconcernedly onto the set.

"Don't you realize," said Taurog, "that I've had all of these people here waiting for you? Where have you been?"

"Oh, I was up all night listening to records," said Mario, yawning. "I'm tired."

"Well, at least you've been learning something," said Taurog. "What records were you listening to?"

Mario looked at Taurog and laughed. "Mine," he said.

It is possible to ascribe another reason for Mario's lateness that day. Mario was often approached by bit players and extras in the cast who hinted that it would be nice if they could get a few additional pay days out of his pictures.

"How about lousing up a scene, or showing up late?" they'd ask him. "Then we can get an extra check for overtime." Terry Robinson insists that Mario obliged the boys and girls now and then. It was the perfect act for Mario on two counts: it gave him a chance to thumb his nose at authority and at the same time to help those less fortunate than himself.

By this time Terry was with Mario almost constantly, living at his big house on Whittier Drive in Beverly Hills, going to fights with him, training him, trying to reason with him about his high living, and, all the while, worshiping his voice. He would often leave the house with Mario early in the morning and remain around the set all day. They would leave the studio together at 8:30 at night, after viewing the day's rushes.

Terry brought his weights around to the set, and during the lunch breaks—nowadays Mario invariably skipped lunch—many of the stars, including Naish, David Niven and even Kathryn Grayson, took turns training with them.

Aware of Mario's bad eye, Terry was astounded when Mario was able to pick out three figures, almost a block away, on a dark sound stage.

"I could hardly see my hand in front of me," says Terry, "and then Mario suddenly said to me, 'I wonder what Sam and Joe and Norman are talking about over there?' He pointed toward the other end of the sound stage. Even with my two good eyes I could scarcely make out the three of them. But the Tiger [Terry's nickname for Mario], with only one good eye, made out Weiler, Pasternak and Taurog as plain as if they were right in front of him."

In addition to "Be My Love," which Ray Sinatra conducted, Mario sang the following numbers in *Toast of New Orleans*:

The "Tina-Lina," another Nicky Brodszky piece; "Boom Biddy Boom Boom"; Bizet's "Flower Song" from *Carmen*; "O Paradis" from *L'Africaine*; "M'apparai" from *Martha*; "I'll Never Love You"; "Bayou Lullaby"; and the duet finale from Act I of *Madama Butterfly*.

As soon as Mario finished the picture, we strongly suspected that Joe Pasternak was going to let nature take its course—that Mario would next be cast in the movie he had to make—*The Great Caruso*.

12. "The Great Caruso"

$\mathcal{T}$HE rolling bass voice, unmistakably that of Ezio Pinza, world-famous star of opera, movies, and South Pacific, rumbled out of the make-up department at M-G-M. It was shortly after 6:30 in the morning, hardly a time, even for Pinza, to be launching into the familiar strains of "Some Enchanted Evening."

Pinza stood listening, his mouth agape. But he wasn't singing. Only a record of Pinza himself could make sounds like these. And Ezio knew it was no record. It was nearly a Perfect imitation of him, and Pinza knew who had to be the performer.

Pinza roared: "Lanza, you son of a bitch, where the hell are you?"

"What did you think of that?" laughed Mario, popping his head into Pinza's room.

A stream of good-natured Italian invective filled the air, unprintable testimonial to Mario's artistry as a mimic.

Mario had always been adept at mimicry. In fact, he was so good at it that his repertoire included Perry Como, Bing Crosby, Frank Sinatra, and a version of Joe Pasternak's soft Hungarian accent that was a local classic.

Acting was another matter. As astute an observer as Clifford Odets commented to Peter Herman Adler, Mario's conductor for *The Great Caruso*, that he was so impressed with Lanza's acting potential he would gladly sign him "as an actor—not a singer." This observation, though not particularly in accord with the general critical assessment of Mario's dramatic abilities, was actually quite perceptive, I think. Many of us close to Mario often felt that his natural instincts for acting might have been better exploited than they were.

However, in *The Great Caruso*, when Mario's talents for acting, mimicry, and singing were put to the test, he emerged as an astounding success, artistically and financially. As Time magazine stated it, he was the "first operatic tenor in history to become a full-blown Hollywood star. He is at once the delight of bobby-soxers, housewives and ordinary song lovers."

Actually Lanza playing Caruso in a film did not seem as natural around M-G-M as it seemed to Mario, his friends and family. Though Mario was proving to be a box office personality after *That Midnight Kiss* and *Toast of New Orleans*, only Louis B. Mayer was convinced that he should be starred in a movie of Caruso's life. That meant trouble, for the long years of Mayer's unquestioned reign at M-G-M were fast drawing to a close. There was a growing schism among the top brass, partially due to the encroachments of television. Nick Schenck, Mayer's boss, now opposed a great many of Mayer's proposals, and one of them he fought tenaciously was Mario as Caruso.

Mayer, for years the M-G-M star maker, had no misgivings about Mario's commercial potentialities, and of course his own opinion had always been sufficient. Now, however, with others at M-C-M not particularly caring if such a picture ever was made at their studio, Mayer had to take the offensive.

When Mario heard of the battle that Mayer was waging in his behalf, he reached L. B. on the phone.

"I want to play Caruso more than anything in the world," he told Mayer, in a thoroughly honest appraisal of his ambitions. "I know you want me to do it, too. If there is anything I can do to help, just tell me."

Now that his rule was being threatened, Mayer welcomed moral support. "Thank you, Mario, my boy," he said, weeping genuine tears. "I will never forget you."

Mayer won out on the issue. It was one of his last victories.

When the news that he would definitely play Caruso reached Mario, he was ecstatic.

"I'll be Caruso every minute of the day," he told me.

The obsession to emulate Caruso, the fantasy of being Caruso, had come to fruition. Now it remained for him to play the part and sing the role, almost as though his destiny were being fulfilled. This was one of the rare occurrences in the entertainment field— or any field, for that matter—where a man actually was given the equipment by God and nature to impersonate an idol. In a sense, and tragically so at the age of thirty, Mario was approaching the climax of his professional and emotional life.

Mario began to study. He read all the books he could find on Caruso, copied his attitudes, his habits, and even his sartorial idiosyncrasies.

"I *am* Caruso now," Mario said, and he felt this and believed it. He even shared Caruso's premonitions of early death. Once when Caruso rinsed his mouth with water before an operatic performance, he was disturbed to notice that the water he spat into the basin was a pinkish red. His wife, Dorothy, did not want to let him continue with his performance. But the great singer was fatalistic, as always.

"Tenors many times die on stage, from hemorrhage, after they sing the big note," said Caruso. He would not be put off by his wife.

Mario's continual fears of dying young, expressed so often to me and to others, could easily have been a further extension of his Caruso fantasy.

Prior to the start of production on *The Great Caruso*, Joe Pasternak was worried about Mario's weight problem. Mario was over 210 pounds at this time, more than he'd been in the actual filming of his first two movies. The decision was made that he should rent Ginger Rogers' ranch in Medford, Oregon, for some six weeks, in an effort to melt off the excess poundage.

Since Mario still exercised his option not to fly, no one flew, Mario, Betty, a Negro butler, and Jack Keller, who was then Mario's press agent, drove to Medford. Under Mario's seat in the car was a large canvas bag with over $500 in silver dollars. Sam Weiler tried to keep money away from Mario, but now Mario could sit there and kick the bag or reach down into it and lovingly feel the silver dollars. Every time he did, he would howl with laughter.

"This was reality for him at last," said Keller. "He couldn't have been more delighted. A check for a million wouldn't have meant as much to him."

At Medford, Mario tortured himself to get his weight down; it was to be the first of many major battles to attack his difficulties. For nearly two months his daily ration consisted mostly of three tomatoes, three hard-boiled eggs, and fruit juice. Occasionally he ate a steak. He did road work in a rubber suit, lifted his weights, shadow boxed, took mercury shots for dehydrating, was up early in the morning and went to bed before ten each night.

When Mario returned to Hollywood to face the cameras for Caruso he had lost 40 pounds and was prepared to deliver a performance that would make him the most talked-about artist in the industry.

Pasternak recalls *Great Caruso*, which was shot in less than eight weeks, as "the smoothest running of all Mario's pictures." But of course, he was speaking in relative terms.

"He got along great with director Richard Thorpe," says Terry Robinson, who was hired as Mario's stand-in for the film.

But even now, as he was realizing a lifelong ambition, Mario seethed with resentment and hostility and the compulsion to drink, to overeat, and to defy authority. There were times when he showed up for work under the influence of alcohol. And there were times when he drank right on the set. He would manage to sneak in his drink or his food in some way, somehow.

Pasternak tells of how Mario would order a mountain of food to be delivered to another star's dressing room. "He wasn't supposed to be eating lunch," says Joe. "But instead of napping as he should have been, he was eating all the food brought in for other actors. He'd walk into a dressing room, sit down, and eat. When he got through, there'd be a graveyard of bones."

Frequently he acted like a potentate, commanding people to do his bidding. For him it was a constant joy; for others, it became impossible. He could be sympathetic and interested in the extras and "the little people" around the studio, yet he could ride them unmercifully, stinging them with insults for minor or nonexistent faults. He could curse a servant, then overtip him. He could be lovable and warm one moment, harsh and unthinking the next. He strutted and posed the way he thought Caruso did. And even off the set he wore the large-sized fedoras and Homburgs that Caruso used to wear, and the spats the master sometimes wore on his trips around the world.

But a strange transformation would come over him when his parents visited the set. Then Mario was instantly on his best behavior.

"I'll sing like you've never heard me sing before, Mom," he'd say to Maria. And as he became her loving little boy again he was almost obsequious with the director, obedient to the conductor, and co-operative with the other players.

Ludwig Donath, the veteran actor of movies, stage, and TV, was one of the few on the set of *Caruso* to win the respect that Mario reserved for his parents. Donath played Alfredo, the man who gave Caruso his first job and later became Caruso's manager.

Donath had often worked with singers on their dramatic roles. And now Mario came to him for advice.

"I wanted nothing from Mario and he could sense that," says Donath. "So he sought me out. He'd say, 'Tell me, Ludwig, what I should do?' He was always careful in my presence to keep out all the four-letter words and to be respectful. Not that I cared. Then I'd go over things with him."

Mario listened carefully to Donath's instructions, whether they had application to Mario's career or his art. But the next day he'd do the direct opposite.

Bombastically, Mario would assert he was Caruso to almost anyone who would listen. But to Donath he refused to make this claim. "He never once said to me he thought he was equal to Caruso or better," recalls Donath. "But he projected himself into the part, perhaps secretly feeling, or at least yearning, to be the rightful successor to his idol."

Donath spent a great deal of time, sometimes as much as three or four hours a day, trying to teach Mario some of the secrets of acting. "Surprisingly, he was not an untalented actor. He had the warmth that one needs, and he loved the world of make-believe. But he didn't know enough about the fundamentals of acting. He never felt secure as an actor, and I guess that complemented his own hidden doubts about his talents as a singer. We would often run through his lines; I would make suggestions as to his interpretation and delivery. I didn't need to teach him gestures or instinctive things about acting; he had these things."

It was part of Peter Herman Adler's strategy to get the most out of Mario's voice by surrounding him in the picture with some of the genuinely great singing talents of the day. Adler informed Pasternak that he should get rid of any mediocrities originally scheduled for the cast and showcase Mario with the best he could find.

So M-G-M hired Blanche Thebom, Giuseppe Valdengo, Dorothy Kirsten, Jarmila Novotna, Gilbert Russell and Nicola Moscona, all of the Metropolitan, as well as the pretty Ann Blyth, to support him. Mario sang fifteen solos and eight numbers in collaboration.

"In my opinion," says Adler today, "I think Mario made mincemeat out of them."

The opera stars themselves, figures in a business notorious for temperament, backbiting, and personality clashes, conceded Mario's brilliance. Some told him he was doing a great service for opera, others acknowledged he was a magnificent tenor.

However, this was not enough to satisfy the troublesome ego of Mario. When it came time for him to sing his numbers he blasted them right at the opera stars. "I'll belt them all down," he told Terry Robinson, "so they won't know what hit them."

Mario made his role a physical thing, especially in his relationships with the opera stars. Nursing a secret dislike for one of the female opera performers, one day during the filming of a duet Mario seized her, slammed her to his chest, then threw her to the floor.

Several days later, when the opera star spied Mario in the street, she started to run after him. Mario was certain she was going to attack him in an effort to even the score. But to his amazement she yelled, "Mario, Mario, that was the greatest scene we played together! It was so real, so emotional!"

Mario was sorely disappointed to learn that the scene had wound up on the cutting room floor.

"After the beating she took," said Mario, "they should've used it."

Some days before *The Great Caruso* opened, M-G-M Night was held at the Hollywood Bowl. Mario was one of the most striking figures on the bill, singing with a youngster named Mary Jane Smith.

After the show, the whole gang went over to Ciro's; Mario went along too, though he had a distaste for Hollywood night life, club hopping, and name dropping. Dean Martin and Jerry Lewis were entertaining that night and, midway through the proceedings, Jerry asked Mario to come up and sing.

Mario obliged by singing "Vesti la giubba." It may be perfectly true that audiences of show business people are generally responsive to one of their own. But Mario outdid himself and so did the audience. Their applause was deafening. Many of them had heard Mario sing before, but it seemed that each time they heard him again their reaction was one of disbelief. He had affected so many people that way in the past—Koussevitzky, Moss Hart, Rosati, Louis B. Mayer.

Then, when the thunderous response stopped, Jerry Lewis faced the audience. "The show's over for the night, folks," he said. "After this what could follow?"

After *The Great Caruso* was finished (the picture bore scant resemblance to Caruso's actual life) Mario was to make his debut on a one-hour radio show for Coca-Cola. Over 1,200 ticket holders lined up outside the CBS Vine Street Playhouse in Hollywood to see and hear him in person. His fame had spread and "The Loveliest Night of the Year," which Mario introduced in this movie, was selling like hot cakes. (Ultimately this was the second best single that Mario ever made for RCA Victor; it sold well over a million copies.)

115

The fans queued up patiently, but their new singing idol failed to put in an appearance. Finally, word was passed along that Mario's unpredictable throat was acting up. However, in an effort to assuage their disappointment, Lanza had arranged to pay the admission for all those who wanted to see his new movie *The Great Caruso*, then on display right around the corner at Hollywood Boulevard's Egyptian Theater.

About half of those in line accepted the invitation and were soon being enthralled by The Great Caruso. If Mario had again disappointed an audience with a needless cancellation, he made up for it with a gracious gesture for which any press agent would have been proud to render his bill.

The Great Caruso opened at New York's Radio City Music Hall in May, 1951, and played through ten incredible weeks, during which time over a million and a half dollars was grossed at that one box office alone. The film eventually earned Mario almost five million dollars from receipts and recording royalties. More than 100,000 Caruso albums were sold before the film was released; and even today there are few record stores that aren't still selling copies.

Among the songs Mario sang in *Great Caruso* were: "Because"; "Celeste Aïda"; "Recitativo" and "Vesti la giubba" from *I Pagliacci*; "M'apparai" from *Martha*; "Ave Maria"; "La donna é mobile"; "Cielo e mar!" from *La Gioconda*; "Mattinata" by Leoncavallo; "La Danza" by Rossini; "A Mare Chiare" by Tosti; "A'Vucchella" by Tosti; "E lucevan le stelle" from *Tosca* by Puccini.

The critics had been slow to warm to Mario's talents in his first two movies, but now they were solidly on his side. Bosley Crowther of *The New York Times* said: "Lanza has an excellent young tenor voice, which he uses with impressive dramatic power."

Otis Guernsey of the New York *Herald Tribune* wrote that "Lanza stands in for the magnificent star as he sings his famous roles in a full and commanding voice. The picture was designed for music lovers."

And *Variety* pitched in with unstinted endorsement:

> The gifted young tenor is definitely on the rise as a popular concert idol. Metro has a natural in Lanza. He's handsome, personable and has a brilliant voice. He's a lyric tenor like Caruso, has his stocky build (he's put on weight since his last picture), his Italianate quality, and some of his flair. His acting conveys something of the simple peasant Caruso essentially was, while his singing is easy, rich, musical and strong. Lanza's talent is obviously of high artistic caliber and quite stirring. The notes are clear, sonorous and ringing. Musically, he's a treat.

A few, like Sigmund Spaeth, writing in *Theatre Arts*, questioned the sincerity of the voice ("the singer concentrates on putting tears into the voice with an exaggerated emotion"). But even Spaeth concluded that Mario's was "by nature an overwhelming voice, with a distinctive personal quality."

Singing like a man possessed, Mario had become, for the eyes and the ears of the music-loving world, the living Caruso. He had once lived to revere and worship Caruso; now millions were adoring and worshiping him as Caruso.

In the record business he was the "boffo" tenor who was "dusting off the turntables." In the movie business he was the man who was indisputably, in 1951, the single most important property in Hollywood. Soon he was to become the most sought-after and applauded singing performer in the concert business.

But Mario's angers and anxieties persisted. He had out-sung and out-shone some of the pre-eminent figures of the Metropolitan itself. Yet, was he really their peer or their superior? Could he really sing in opera? Would he fail dismally outside of motion pictures?

As George London once remarked some years later: "The continual conflict within Mario was his desire to keep on earning the unbelievable sums of money that came his way overnight in Hollywood and his need to be accepted, recognized and appreciated as the world's greatest singer, opera or otherwise."

Mario was terribly sensitive about this dichotomy in his desires and needs. When London visited the Coast shortly after Mario's success in *Caruso*, he found that it would be impossible for him to keep an appointment with his old friend. George phoned Mario. "I'm sorry," he said, "but I just can't make it. Let's make it another time."

Seething over this rejection—unplanned and unpremeditated on London's part—Mario lashed out at his "tormentor." "I'm a greater star than you are," he cried. "*You* can't brush *me* off!"

But the continued reservations of his venerable teaching master, Enrico Rosati, hurt Mario more than anything else. Mario was convinced of his urgent need for Rosati's advice and encouragement. He called the old man from Hollywood.

"I need you badly, Maestro," pleaded Mario. "Come with me to Hollywood. You can teach me so much that I must still learn."

Rosati had no desire to hurt his former student—the disciple who had failed him, despite his movie riches and international fame.

"My boy," Rosati answered, "I never followed Gigli or Melton or Volpi or any of the others. Why should I follow you? So I will not come to you. But keep remembering one thing always, as long as you sing, and wherever you are, you must work and work and work."

Mario remained silent. He was stung and disappointed.

Then Rosati finished: "You must know in your heart, now, you are not yet Caruso. You may never be Caruso."

13. Raphaela

RAPHAELA FASANO was a radiant, effervescent little girl of ten in 1951. She lived with her mother, her father—a refrigerator repairman—two brothers and three sisters at Seth Boyden Village in Newark, New Jersey.

Raphaela was a popular child and she had her youthful beaux in the neighborhood. But there was a man living many miles away, in Hollywood, California, with whom she was really in love; his name was Mario Lanza. From the first time she heard him sing, she adopted him as her secret sweetheart. It was common knowledge in the Fasano household that Raphaela's heart belonged only to this man.

Then a catastrophe befell Raphaela and her family. She became ill of Hodgkin's disease, and the doctors did not hold out much hope that she would live more than a few months. So Mrs. Fasano, seeking to bring some happiness and laughter into Raphaela's ebbing life, thought of Mario Lanza and how much the great singer meant to her little girl. On an impulse, and fully expecting to be thwarted in her efforts, she picked up the phone one morning and called California.

Terry Robinson reached the phone ahead of Mario. Mrs. Fasano blurted out to him the story of the misfortune that had descended on the Fasano family, and Terry listened quietly.

"Would it be asking too much of Mr. Lanza if he just talked to my Raphaela on the phone?" asked Mrs. Fasano.

"I'll tell Mario about it," promised Terry. "I'm sure you'll be hearing from him."

When Mrs. Fasano hung up her phone in Newark she never expected to hear from Mario. It was simply too much to expect that he would concern himself with the unhappiness of a poor family in New Jersey, and with the suffering of a child he had never seen.

But she did not know the side of Mario that those of us close to him had come to love. With all of his faults, with all of his hostilities and imperfections, Mario still managed to be one of the warmest, most sympathetic humans I have ever seen. I once saw him cry when he passed a blind man in the street. When he talked on the long-distance phone with his daughter Colleen, his greatest fan, tears would often form in his eyes and he would say to me, "Costa, why don't we go right home, so I can kiss my little girl?" The night of one of his movie openings, he waited at home with Colleen in his arms, and when Terry called to tell him how the

122

audience had reacted to his work, he cried as he hugged and kissed Colleen till she could hardly breathe. When his mother was removed to a Philadelphia hospital for a kidney operation, he kept her room smothered in flowers. But he couldn't bear to see her sick, or in pain.

Mario did much more than contact Mrs. Fasano. He suggested at once to Terry and Betty that Raphaela be invited to come out to visit with him. "I want Raphaela to be with us before Christmas comes," he said. Then he phoned the Fasano home in New Jersey, and while a bed-fast youngster listened as she had never listened to anything else before, he sang to her. For over ten minutes Mario poured his heart into "Silent Night" and other Christmas songs. And the little child with the wan face listened, her dark eyes glowing with joy.

When the special concert was at an end, Mario's voice nearly broke with emotion. "I didn't know whether I would make it or not," he said. "I could see that darling little kid in bed, and I knew she was dying. And around me, while I sang, were my own little girls. It was almost too much for me to take. But if Raphaela could take it, I guess I could."

Naturally the story of Mario's deed hit the newspapers, and I suppose that most people who read about it were convinced the whole thing was created, produced and directed by some Hollywood press agent. This is an injustice to Mario and far from the truth.

Mario's gesture set off an amazing chain reaction. A New York newspaper arranged Raphaela's trip; an airline flew her out to California with her mother and a nurse as guests; and a hotel in downtown Los Angeles gave the Fasano party one of the finest rooms in the house, courtesy of two anonymous New York businessmen who had read about the private long-distance concert Mario had sung for the child. For five days Raphaela had the time of her young life, which, despite all the efforts of medical science, was destined to be terminated in a year. She visited Mario on the set of *Because You're Mine*, which he had begun to work on at this time, and played at Mario's house in Beverly Hills with his children and the children of Jerry Lewis, Ricardo Montalban, and Kathryn Grayson.

Until Raphaela died, Mario remained her most ardent admirer. Scarcely a week went by that he didn't call New Jersey and talk to her. Almost every Friday the phone would ring in the Fasano home and the operator would say: "Hollywood calling." Then Mario would greet his "sweetheart" with a cheery hello and a song. When he wasn't singing to her, Mario sent her gifts—records, dolls, flowers, candy.

Unaware that Raphaela had died the day before, Mario called as usual on Friday, January 30, 1953. Louis Fasano, Raphaela's partly invalided father, answered the phone.

"I'm sorry," said Mr. Fasano, "but Raphaela will not be able to listen to you any more, Mr. Lanza. She died yesterday. She wanted so much to hear you again. But she just couldn't make it."

When Raphaela was buried in the Holy Cross Cemetery, one of Mario's last presents—a sterling silver Immaculate Conception Medal—was around her neck.

During the next few years Mario never forgot poor Raphaela. To this day, now that Mario and Betty have both joined Raphaela in death, Mrs. Fasano still corresponds with the Cocozzas.

"My little Raphaela was in love with Mario," Mrs. Fasano says. "The trip was like a dream come true for her. It's so wonderful that she could have it before she left us."

When Sam Weiler suggested a leisurely four-day trip to Hawaii on the steamship *Lorelei*, Mario was ecstatic. He had never been on an ocean liner before. That, combined with the fact that he felt he had earned a good vacation, put him in high spirits for the trip.

His parents and some of his friends came down to the dock to see him off. The weather was just right for the sailing. In addition, Tyrone Power and his beautiful wife, Linda Christian, were on board, and Mario was pleased at the prospect of spending time with them.

Once out at sea, Mario made an alarming discovery: aside from the Powers, most of the passengers were elderly. At once he began roaming the decks looking for youthful faces. "This boat is like an old folks home," he roared. But soon he found great delight in flirting with older women, tickling their vanity and causing the kind of minor commotion that people on a vacation seem to enjoy. However, it was Ty whom the passengers were more interested in. This was probably the only time in his life that Mario took second place to another celebrity. But he really didn't mind; he was quite fond of Power.

We stayed at the Royal Hawaiian Hotel in Honolulu. It is right on Waikiki Beach, but Mario never once went into the water. He was busy rehearsing for his recording sessions, promoting his movies, attending luncheons and giving interviews to the press. He also did three concerts at the local high school auditorium. These had been booked for him by Sam Weiler before we left.

Mario immediately attended a luau. The pig was wonderful; but he didn't particularly care for another favorite Hawaiian dish called poi, which resembles pea soup in appearance and happens to contain about 150 calories per cup. However, he had no desire to insult the Hawaiians, who had, till that time, treated him elegantly. So he downed his portion of poi.

"Che bellezza!" he exclaimed, licking his fingers with simulated relish. This promptly netted him another portion, which he also downed manfully. Mario was a consummate actor, even at the dinner table.

Then to top off the evening, Mario sang "O Sole Mio" to the accompaniment of a lone guitar. Singing outdoors, with the wind gently whispering through the trees, Mario rewarded his listeners with a melting performance. I have rarely heard him in better voice or seen him in better spirits. Perhaps he should have remained in this enchanting atmosphere forever.

A few nights later the Powers threw a luau at their villa in Honolulu. It rained heavily and the poor pig was practically drowned, but it still tasted good. Mario sang, at Ty's request. Ty was so pleased he went swimming in the pool with his watch on in the early hours of the morning. At five in the morning Linda fixed us bacon and eggs; the food, at that hour, was almost as delicious a sight as she was.

For Mario's last concert in Hawaii the local manager asked him to sing the famous song of the islands, "Aloha." Mario realized he didn't know the number and would have to learn it in twenty-four hours, and the verse was rather difficult to pick up in such a short time. This was the only incident during our Hawaiian siesta that caused Mario any concern or upset.

"Why don't you do a duet with me?" he said. "It'll be the first time in history an accompanist ever joined a singer like this."

It wasn't, but I agreed. We were some combination!

Then our holiday in Hawaii drew to a close, to the sorrow of all of us—the Weilers, the Pasternaks, the Lanzas, and myself. It was time to go home to prepare for another tour, one that Sam felt would be of immense importance, financially and artistically, to Mario.

I have often seen the tour referred to as the "Lanza Bonanza." At least that was what Terry liked to call it.

It was actually *The Great Caruso* tour.

In many ways, it was the climax of Mario's career.

Callinicos and Mario at first RCA Victor recording session, 1949

Mario and family, 1949

Kathryn Grayson and Mario in THE TOAST OF NEW ORLEANS

Mario with Ann Blyth (right) and Dorothy Kirsten in THE GREAT CARUSO

Mario at two

Mario as a G.I.,1943

The Bel Canto Trio—George London, Frances Yeend, and Mario

Mario and Betty in New York, 1946

Philadelphia neighbors welcome Mario home during premiere of
THAT MIDNIGHT KISS

Terry Robinson with Mario

THE QUEEN GREE
MARIO LANZA .

*Mario with Tyrone Power, Linda Christian, Joe Pasternak and wife, Betty
Lanza, and Constantine Callinicos in Honolulu, Spring, 1950*

Mario with Italian actor Renato Raschel, Colleen, and Elissa (back), Rome, 1958

Mario as Otello in SERENADE

14. Triumphant Tour

$\mathscr{I}$F YOU had seen and heard what went on in twenty-two cities from Scranton, Pennsylvania, to Fresno, California, during the months of February, March and April of 1951, you would then understand the ambivalent attitudes performers have toward their public. I was there, I saw it, I heard it. I was touched by it, often offended by it, and almost maimed by it from time to time. And mind, my name was not Mario Lanza.

"Caruso himself never commanded the adulation that swamped Lanza on his latest concert tour," claimed *Time* magazine in the August 1951 issue that featured Mario's picture on the cover.

From the day the tour began, Mario was besieged by young and old, the shy and bold, the diffident and daring. They begged for autographs, peeped through the keyholes of his hotel rooms, grabbed at the scarf or the tie around his neck, seized scraps of food from his mouth in public restaurants. There was a continual cater-wauling and din in his ears. "Mario, we love you, you're wonderful!" "Let me kiss you, Mario!" Everywhere Mario went his fans—mostly women—were not far behind. Leaving theaters was a problem. Entering a hotel was worse. Going to sleep was impossible. We had to devise all sorts of ruses to throw the maniacal, frenzied fans off our tracks. Sometimes it worked, more often it didn't.

To remain in one piece, in reasonably good humor, while being stripped, crushed, choked and gouged, was a continual challenge to Mario during these hectic days. He came through it slightly out of breath, more than a little bewildered by his impact on the mass imagination; but chances are he could not have come through it at all without the rigid physical conditioning Terry put him through just before the tour began.

Some weeks after our return from Hawaii Sam Weiler took a look at Mario's bulging waistline, then at the schedule of twenty-three bookings that Columbia Artists had lined up for us, and decided it was high time to get down to business. He proposed at once a training trip to Palm Springs.

Mario objected, insisting he could get himself in shape easily enough. But neither he nor anyone else believed it: he had suffered through three crash programs to make three movies; and now he was heavier than ever—encased in suet. He'd have to lose at least fifty pounds to resemble the Mario Lanza that his fans knew.

Still, Mario did not want to train. He felt he had reached his peak: he was the country's premier recording star; his latest movie was breaking records everywhere; he had received $100,000 for *Great Caruso*. On any terms he was an unqualified success.

Then why couldn't he relax and enjoy his success? Why couldn't he indulge his fondness for food and drink? He'd earned everything; he'd toed the line for everyone. So now, he thought, let them take him as he was—or not at all.

What Mario chose to ignore was the very nature of a performer's art, that he must earn his success continually, over and over again in each song, record, concert, and film. His fears and insecurities ruled him more strongly than ever; food and drink were his escapes from judgment.

The beer drinking, the pizza snacks, the nightly feasts of Chinese food at home, the parties at D'Amore's place on Las Palmas Street—these were putting the weight on him, trapping him in his own bulk. And the more food and drink that went down, the less energy and desire Mario had for work.

Sam called me one morning. "I'm afraid if something isn't done with Mario, quick, we'll have to call off the tour."

"We can't call it off," I said. "He knows he must do it."

"I know, Costa," said Sam wearily. "But take one look at him and you'll know he can't do it. He's eating his way out of the business." Then, knowing that I was relying on income from the tour, Sam assured me of some payment even if plans had to be canceled.

I refused to take a settlement, insisting Mario was capable of making the tour. When I hung up, I was almost limp with anger, not only at the prospect of a money loss, but also at the thought of how close Mario was to destroying a career that was now at a new high.

I was invited to move in with the Cocozzas, who were then living in an apartment on South Crescent Drive. They said they would be willing to put me up until Mario was ready to do the tour. A few days went by without a single word from Mario or Sam.

Then one day Mario called. "I want to go to Palm Springs to chop some weight off," he said, somewhat sheepishly. "Don't worry, we'll do this tour!"

I was delighted with my victory, as ephemeral as it turned out to be.

In mid-January, 1951, we left by car for Palm Springs. Sam, Betty and Mario went down in Sam's Cadillac and Terry and I followed in the Oldsmobile, with all of the equipment and baggage. It didn't take us long to find a three-bedroom ranch house secluded from the town, surrounded by desert and mountains. If a man couldn't relax, train and study in this setting, he would never be able to do it anywhere on earth.

The undisciplined Mario turned overnight into a Spartan. He showed incredible willpower and an honest desire to lose weight. He ate little more than boiled eggs, tomatoes, grapefruit, skimmed milk, tangelos, the once-a-day rare roast beef and steak and yogurt and wheat germ. We dieted, too, rather than tantalize Mario with food forbidden to him. We were in bed by ten and up by seven.

From eight o'clock in the morning, when Mario was out with Terry, running, hiking, and climbing, till late in the afternoon, it was all business, all preparation for the ordeal ahead. Since there were just three weeks to the Scranton date on February 16, Mario could not let up. He had to lose at least two and a half pounds every day for twenty-one days in order to get down below 200. Mario and I were at the piano each morning from 10 to 11; from

4 to 5 in the afternoon, when the heat of the day—sometimes over 105—had tapered off a bit, we worked again. He was inspired now. It was remarkable to see a man who had descended almost to the level of an animal suddenly reverse his course and act with maturity, responsibility, and self-abnegation.

One day, as we walked in the desert in our heavy rubber sweat suits, I said to Mario, "I don't know why I'm doing this, but it's the greatest thing in the world for you."

"This is the only way to live, Costa. The healthy road is the right road," Mario said.

There was no doubt that in those few moments Mario believed what he said, and believed it strongly. The great misfortune was his utter inability to live out his beliefs and his promises to himself and others.

During the day Mario would spar with Terry, who insisted, along with former heavyweight champ Rocky Marciano, that he could have been a fine boxer. Mario enjoyed the simple violence of the sport. He also enjoyed painting pictures in his spare time. But the household reflected Mario's grim determination to get in shape, and for those twenty-one days the conversation seldom drifted from the subject of music and diet.

Some fifty pounds lighter, and with buoyant spirits, Mario left Palm Springs on February 11. Five days later the tour opened in Scranton, then weaved its hectic, exuberant way through Utica, New York; Baltimore; Richmond, Virginia; Pittsburgh; Columbus, Ohio; Philadelphia; Miami Beach; Orlando, Florida; Daytona Beach, Florida; Tampa; New Orleans; Milwaukee; Chicago; St. Louis (two concerts were booked in one day here and Mario missed one, the only cancellation of the whole junket); Toledo; Cincinnati; Wichita; Kansas City; Omaha, Nebraska; Ogden, Utah; and

Fresno, California. It was box office and bedlam every step of the way.

Assuring its readers this was the most successful "long-hair" tour since Nelson Eddy's some ten years before. *Variety* headlined that LANZA PROVES HOTTEST DRAW WITH $177,720 GROSS IN 22 CONCERTS. The only other tours that matched it, the newspaper went on to say, were Sadler's Wells Ballet, the Toscanini-NBC Symphony, and the Royal Philharmonic.

Mario's average fee for each concert was over $4,500. In some cities—Milwaukee, where he pulled down $6,750, Omaha where he received $6,180, and New Orleans, where his take was over $6,000-Mario surpassed the fees paid any artist before, and probably since. These figures, in the concert business, are truly formidable. No doubt they led Sam Weiler, as well as executives of Columbia Artists, to dream of putting Mario into arenas that could accommodate even larger crowds. It never worked out that way.

Even before Mario ever sang a note on the tour, we sensed what we were in for when we arrived in Scranton. Mario was scheduled to visit a local department store to autograph some of his record albums. When he arrived, there were more women in the store, outside of it, and coming to it than I had ever seen before in my life.

At first Mario joked about it: "What a harem I could pick up around here!" But as we started for the record department, the trouble began. The women clutched for Mario, screeched his name, mauled him, tried to tackle him.

"I thought Times Square was rough, but this takes the cake," said Mario as he was swept along by the mob.

Then the girls started to stand on the counters to get a better look at their hero. Furniture, washing machines, radio cabinets, and desks became grandstand and bleacher seats.

"Sing for us, Mario," they yelled. And if he had, he couldn't have been heard two feet away, even with the biggest voice in the world. "Hey, be my love, Mario!" . . . "Kiss me, Mario!"

The crush became so dangerous that the police and firemen were called into action by the store owners. When order was temporarily restored, Mario managed to get a pen out of his pocket and sign his name a few times. But then the mob took over again.

On the stage before 5,567 people that night, Mario shamelessly plugged his latest records and used the overhead handclasp of a fighter to acknowledge applause. His only concession to orthodoxy was his tux and black tie. That afternoon and that evening had set the pattern for the whole tour.

In Richmond, Virginia, the local concert hall was jammed with over 4,000 people. Back at our hotel we found that a convention of Southern physical education instructors was in progress, and when the girls found that Mario was staying at the same hotel they settled in the hall outside his room and wouldn't leave. Around three in the morning they were still tittering and squealing outside the door, and Mario had had enough.

"Let's start a fire in the hotel," said Mario wearily.

"That wouldn't help at all," I answered. "They'd only come running to you to be rescued."

When we hit Pittsburgh for our March 6 concert, we hadn't been in the lobby of the William Penn Hotel more than a minute when two burly gentlemen approached us.

"You're gonna need some protection in this town," one of them said to Mario.

"Protection from what?" said Mario. "From kissing and hugging? Hell, I love every second of it!"

"Well, don't say we didn't warn you."

The men, who turned out to be local detectives, knew their territory well.

The Syria Mosque, the largest hall in Pittsburgh, had sold out its 3,800 tickets so fast that Edward Specter, the Pittsburgh Symphony manager, decided to sell tickets to Mario's afternoon rehearsal. As far as anyone knows, the idea was unprecedented; not even Mario had tried it. Specter placed ads in the morning newspapers:

Due to the fact that the Pittsburgh Symphony Concert on Tuesday evening, March 6, with Mario Lanza as soloist, has been completely sold out, and because of the continued and overwhelming demand for tickets, the rehearsal for this concert will be open to the public at general admission prices.

The tickets went almost as fast as they had for the regular program.

Mario worked his way through the shouting, frenzied crowds outside the Mosque. Inside he found an audience that surpassed anything he had ever seen in the past. Bobby-soxers had played hookey to attend. They raised a sustained wailing such as I had never heard before. They were so noisy and unruly that special detectives had to be assigned to different sections of the hall to keep order. When Mario sang they managed to remain quiet. But when he stopped for an instant, the cacophony rose again. They became so unmanageable that the rehearsal conductor, Vladimir Bakaleini-koff, turned and warned them to be quiet.

"This is a symphony orchestra," he scolded. "I insist that you be very respectful. *Shut up!*"

Bakaleinikoff s plea worked—for about two minutes. Then the noise started up again. On a sudden impulse, Mario lobbed his handkerchief into the crowd. A wild melee ensued.

The next night the regular concert took place. There were several hundred more people in the theater than it officially held. On this evening Terry Robinson, who frequently sold souvenir programs at fifty cents a copy, set his all-time record. There were fewer bobby-soxers in the audience, but no less of a din. Mario loved it.

It amused Mario to help Terry sell programs. He would walk to the center of the stage, raise his arms for quiet, then give the pitch.

"Ladies and gentlemen, we have a stack of encore requests *this* high," and he'd gesture with his hands. "I'd like to do many of them for you. But you have to do something for me first. Tonight is the birthday of my good friend, Terry Robinson. He's that nice-looking boy who is selling programs in the lobby. Why don't you be nice and buy a program from him?"

Terry had more birthdays during the Big Tour than a piano has keys. However, when we hit Columbus it actually was Terry's birthday—March 9. This time Mario not only encouraged the crowd of over 3,500, squeezed into 3,200 seats in Memorial Hall, to buy Terry's programs, but he also announced that he was going to sing "Because" in honor of his buddy.

"The son of a gun brought tears to my eyes," recalls Terry. "I don't think I ever heard him sing as well."

On March 12 our happy, beleaguered caravan arrived at the Ritz Carlton Hotel in Philadelphia. The next night Mario was to sing at the Academy of Music, where Serge Koussevitzky had first heard him.

Mario was hailed as a hero, but as always he reacted strangely to his hometown. He continued to insist that Philadelphia had shown him little regard, though he never said what he expected. Perhaps one episode explains it: Mario had once granted a rather lurid interview to a magazine writer and spun out a story of dodging gangster bullets in his youth. When the story appeared, many of the citizens of South Philadelphia felt that Mario had done their neighborhood a grave injustice. In retaliation, they plastered some tomatoes on Salvatore Lanza's windows and destroyed a few of Mario's records in a vindictive public ceremony.

This time, of course, the South Philadelphians were wearing their best company manners. They crowded in front of the Lanza house on Mercy Street, ignored Mayor Bernard Samuel, who had cut short his work at City Hall to be on hand for the homecoming celebration, and made Mario arm-weary with requests for autographs. Mario managed to duck out of the formal ceremonies for a few minutes to visit with his old friend Nicky Petrella, proprietor of a record shop just up the street.

Back at the Ritz Carlton, Mario tried to relax for a while with Terry and George Eiferman, "Mr. America." Terry, Mario, and George were tying into a seafood dinner when Manny Sacks, vice-president of RCA, knocked on the door.

Mario had expected him and had alerted George to strip down to the waist and answer the door.

When Manny was greeted by George, he almost fell over.

"I guess I have the wrong room," Manny said.

Then, in a booming bass voice, Mr. America said, "Follow me."

George directed Manny into the next room, where Mario and Terry were beside themselves with joy over the incident.

"He's my new butler," howled Mario.

Lanza's humor was always of that kind—simple and unsubtle, but generally not quite that harmless. Practical jokers often end up doling out physical punishment to others, and Mario was no exception.

At the Academy of Music concert the scale was the usual $5 top for seats. But many tickets had fallen into the hands of scalpers. I had heard that some seats sold for as high as $40 and $50. But this was the case throughout the whole tour, even in Omaha, where the concert took place in an auditorium that seated close to 10,000. No one who heard Mario in Omaha would ever again lend credence to the rumor that the bigness of Mario's voice could be attributed to sound engineers. Mario had so much power that at no time during the tour did he use a microphone.

Excited by the adulation of the crowds, eager to continue pleasing them, Mario held his appetite carefully in check. He ate sparingly. He showed no inclination to duck a performance, and though the demands on his time and patience were great and continual, he took it each day and came back for more. Whatever had changed him from a sloth into a responsible artist, the change was remarkable.

At least in one respect, however, Mario had not changed. Before each concert it was a taut, tense man who confronted me. Then and between songs I tried to give him the reassurance he needed so desperately.

"You're in better voice tonight than ever before," I'd tell him. Even if you repeat that to a man one hundred times, he must be told it another hundred times—especially if the artist's name is Mario Lanza.

Mario might turn to me after a selection. "How did that sound, Costa? How was the C?"

"You've never had trouble with your high notes, Mario. Go to it, you're killing them."

In return, Mario was always thoughtful and generous with me, always respected my talents and supported me with lavish praise.

"You're terrific tonight," he'd say. "What a team!"

A pianist doesn't always receive this kind of support from an artist.

Though I was practically as anonymous as a waiter in this situation, it became increasingly clear that I did have a certain importance to Mario. He needed my patience, enthusiasm and encouragement, and he also needed me to carry half of the 59-minute show with my piano solos. If the fans had come to hear Mario and had paid to hear Mario, it was still up to me to hold their attention during those ordinarily restless moments when Mario was taking his breather. I think I did this job fairly satisfactorily.

As I look back on the tour—the shouting crowds; the police in each city trying to keep Mario from being crushed, robbed of his handkerchiefs, ties, and scarves; the continual procession of official greeters and welcoming ceremonies, which Mario always abhorred; the endless questions from reporters; the waiting after the concert for the crowds to disappear (it was midnight usually before we could sneak back to our hotel); the never-ending tumult, the keyhole-peeping dressing room intrusions—Mario exceeded my fondest hopes.

Physically, he remained at his best. Slimmed down, vigorous and athletic in his manner, elegantly attired in dark blue suit, black form-fitting overcoat, gray Homburg, blue tie with gold stripes, black shoes, gray socks, gray gloves, gray muffler, Mario would have been attractive in any crowd. With the voice and center stage, he was truly magnificent.

When a man earns over $100,000 for less than three months of singing, when he stays at the country's most luxurious hotels, when he eats the finest steaks daily, when the public applauds his every gesture and reacts to each of his groans and grimaces, there is hardly any reason to suspect he is suffering any excruciating agony. Yet, notwithstanding the success and acclaim that inundated him, Mario was never truly happy.

Aside from the self-doubts that continually assailed him, Mario still lacked—and never developed—a mature perspective on his position as a celebrity. He didn't understand his obligation to his fans. His concept of this obligation was limited to the autographs he signed assiduously and the moments he gladly permitted himself to be a target in a wild rush. And he could never accept the isolation that was forced on him after he was through singing.

"Why do I have to spend my whole life behind closed doors, like a guy in stir?" Mario once said to Sam Weiler.

"The only way I can try to explain it," Sam said, "is that if someone came along and gave me a million dollars in a vase, I wouldn't carry the vase around, because it might break and my money would blow away. You've got a million-dollar throat. What should you do? Go out among people? Strain your voice? No, you've got to protect it, baby it—all the time."

Mario grudgingly submitted to his isolation. But he rebelled against it inwardly. Considering the kind of a man he was, it had to take a great deal out of him to accept the inactivity and loneliness. Sitting in his hotel room—which he practically never left, except to keep his concert dates—he had too much time to brood, to think about himself, to let the nagging doubts consume him, to rage at the torments of the heretical critics, to invent enemies and doubt his friends.

During the *Caruso* tour, he considered himself the highest paid prisoner in the world.

15. "Because You're Mine"

THE late afternoon rays of the California sun slanted through the Venetian blinds in Joe Pasternak's roomy office at the M-G-M studios. After minutes of silent pacing the producer stopped, pointed a bony finger in the direction of Mario Lanza, and pleaded, "Just tell me what you want!"

Mario, still sporting the Homburg, spats and cane that were a trademark since The Great Caruso, had been carrying on a running dispute with Pasternak about his next movie. He stood, red-faced and petulant, in front of Pasternak's desk.

"You tell me what's next," said Mario, "and I'll tell you what I think about it."

151

For some time, Pasternak's plan for Mario's future was to make a picture about a great singer who is drafted into the United States Army and, despite his hatred for the life, learns to accept it and becomes a better man for the experience. Although the projected movie bore a certain resemblance to Mario's own background, Pasternak did not entirely conceive of it as a biographical effort. Rather, he thought it would serve to postpone, for a time, the inevitable big opera picture that he had in mind for Mario. "I didn't want him set in the public consciousness as an opera star," Pasternak wrote in his book, *Easy the Hard Way*. "I wanted him to be taken also as a man."

Pasternak thought now was as good a time as any to reveal his plans to Mario. He ran through the plot, then said, "I think it would be a natural for your talents. Your fans would love you in it, as a plain GI. It's only a few years since the war, and the GI role would be a very sympathetic one for you."

"Are you serious?" said Mario instantly. "How can you put Caruso in the Army? I don't think Mario Lanza will ever do it."

"Do you want to play God?" Pasternak shouted. "I'll get you the rights."

That finished the interview for the day. Mario stormed out of Pasternak's office convinced he was being miscast, mishandled, maltreated. The producer watched him go, convinced Mario was a spoiled ingrate with a monstrous ego.

Pasternak's movie was made under the title *Because You're Mine*. Mario had attacked the story as "junk," and junk it may have been; but though it stood forewarned, the studio was not prepared for the unending series of battles and hardships that ensued.

Mario ate ravenously and continuously. He disapproved of Doretta Morrow, who played James Whitmore's sister in the movie, and let it show in his love scenes with her. And he drank—heavily.

Pasternak searched in vain for ways to appeal to Mario's good sense. The services of the beloved Jimmy Durante were solicited in an effort to curb Mario's excesses. But even Jimmy, whom Mario liked and respected, met a stone wall of resistance. Nothing could quell the fire in Mario.

Everything he did—and didn't do—reflected his vicious state of mind. After our *Caruso* tour I had written "You Are My Love," a ballad with lyrics by Paul Francis Webster, who had also written the lyrics for "The Loveliest Night of the Year." At the start Mario had made it clear that he was anxious to record the song. But he kept postponing, ignoring, and forgetting. If the delay temporarily held back my career and a $2,000 advance (from a New York publishing company), I felt certain Mario was not hurting me deliberately. But there was real malice in his tantrums, his eating and drinking: at one point they held up shooting on *Because You're Mine* for almost six weeks and cost M-G-M dearly.

Behind Mario's fierce and sullen mood there was a new personal problem; he began to realize that he was not quite as rich as he thought he should be, considering he made over a million dollars in 1951. He had paid the federal government $425,000 in taxes for the year, but he felt there should be plenty left over to give to his parents, to entertain his friends, to live the lavish life to which he had grown accustomed.

When it seemed that some of Sam Weiler's investments had not turned out as advantageously as Mario thought they should, his naturally suspicious nature was inflamed. He made accusations that even friendship could not tolerate.

An agreement was drawn up between Mario and Sam which gave Weiler five percent of Mario's earnings for the next eleven years. With that, Mario terminated all their dealings.

Now in Mario's twisted mind everyone was suspect and every remark made to him was misconstrued.

One day Joe Pasternak mentioned to Mario that he was about to sell his $145,000 house in luxurious Bel-Air.

"What does the house cost?" Mario asked.

"I paid $145,000 for it," said Pasternak. "I'll take $145,000."

"Here," Mario said. He pulled out a wad of money—$25,000 in cash, Pasternak insists.

"Look, Mario," said Joe. "I don't want your money. If you like the house, speak to Betty, get the house appraised, talk to your lawyers about it. This is no small matter. Get some good advice."

So matters stood for two days. The next Pasternak heard was that Mario was accusing him of trying to steal his $25,000.

"That's the way things went with Mario," says Pasternak. "At first, he was delighted that I had the house for sale, then he appreciated my consideration for him and his money, and the next thing I knew I was involved in some deep dark plot to take his money away from him. I have the feeling some of his reactions were not wholly his own, and that he was put up to it by someone else, perhaps his wife. But that always was one of his misfortunes—lack of guidance. Everything was a conspiracy against him. Suspicion made him terribly sick. It was awful to watch, terrible, to go through the heartaches and pain with him."

Mario's hostility toward Pasternak became so intense that once he rammed his Cadillac into the mailbox in front of Pasternak's home. Another time, when he had been drinking heavily, he paid a nocturnal call on the Pasternak home and stood out front bellowing threats to assault Joe and his wife.

If Mario believed in his heart that nobody could be trusted, he still came to me for help, at least professionally. While he was making *Because You're Mine*, he called me at six one morning from Hollywood. I had returned to New York to fulfill other obligations, and, considering Mario's negligent attitude toward my record, I hadn't expected to hear from him.

His voice sounded tired and strained on the phone. "I need your help, Costa. You've got to come out here to conduct my operatic material and my Neapolitan stuff. I'm just not singing right."

I told him I'd come.

At nine the same morning Jimmy Melton called and asked me if I'd go on tour with him. I wanted to help Mario very badly, and yet I wanted the assignment with Melton. I told him of my promise to go out to Mario at once. When Melton agreed to pay my transportation expenses to and from Hollywood to all the engagements on his tour, I told him I'd work with him, too.

I flew to Hollywood to see what was ailing Mario. It took me three days to get there because of stormy conditions that held up the flights. When I arrived in California I met a Mario who looked thin, wan, and distraught. Even his voice was thin; the old ring of bravado was gone. He was thin from excessive dieting, and now, oddly, he was having trouble trying to regain some of the fifty-odd pounds he had managed finally to shed for *Because You're Mine*.

"You won't believe this," he said to me, "but my appetite is gone. I can't eat a thing."

This boy was in terrible trouble; he knew it and I knew it. But I also knew nothing would be done, or could be done. Psychiatry, the solution that now seemed so obvious, could not be suggested to Mario by a friend. And when it was suggested to Betty, she flatly refused to have anything to do with the idea. Even when Mario became violent and brutal in his behavior, Betty could not face or understand the fact that he was terribly sick.

Finally, taking their lives in their hands, Terry Robinson and his friend Lloyd Shearer, a West Coast writer, made an attempt to obtain help for Mario. It was, in Terry's words, a "harrowing experience."

Terry and Shearer chartered a private plane to bring Mario to New York, where it was their intention to have him examined by a psychiatrist at a clinic for nervous disorders.

The flight was a nightmare. Mario had been drinking steadily and was not in the least in accord with the plan. He fought with his two friends, cursed them, swore to get them and everybody else who said there was something wrong with him. When the plane landed with its strange cargo, Mario was literally dragged to an apartment in mid-Manhattan, where he remained, under guard, until arrangements could be made to have him speak to the psychiatrist.

After three hours of examination by the psychiatrist, Mario bolted out of the room. Panting like an enraged beast, he encountered Terry and Shearer in the corridor of the hospital.

"What are you trying to do to me?" he shouted at the top of his lungs. "This doctor is crazy. I know more about him than he knows about me! Let me out of here! Nobody can keep me in this booby hatch. I'm Mario Lanza!"

The psychiatrist could do nothing to force Mario to stay. Obviously, Mario had neither the desire to subject himself to treatment nor the self-discipline to go through with a prolonged period of mental therapy. However, the doctor was convinced that Mario had lost touch with reality, that he needed help desperately.

In later years, when Mario's mental and physical condition became increasingly aggravated, he paid a dozen visits to Dr. Augustus Rose, the head of the Neurology Department at UCLA. It was just a start, and a poor one. Dr. Rose needed much more time and cooperation from Mario than he ever succeeded in getting.

"I can't say with any assurance," Dr. Bose said, after Mario died, "whether sustained therapy would ever have helped this man."

In spite of the miasma surrounding it, and with the help of constant strategy meetings, conferences, prolonged persuasion, intermittent severity and coddling, *Because You're Mine* was finally completed. And amazingly enough, Mario's singing was still in a class by itself.

The sad turmoil that beset the star of the movie was inadvertently revealed in a paragraph of *Variety's* review, which appeared in September, 1952. "Lanza slimmer than in *Caruso*. Sometimes seems heavier. Reminder of long delay in making film while Lanza made weight."

But the same reviewer had only admiration for his artistry: "Terrific Lanza singing."

Otis L. Guernsey, Jr., of the New York *Herald Tribune*, commented that "Mario sings with all the vigor and expression that have made him one of the most popular phenomena of the modem musical screen."

In addition to Nicky Brodszky's newest hit, *Because You're Mine*, Mario sang "Granada" ("Lanza really lets his voice give out," raved *Variety* about this number); "O Paradis" from the opera *L'Africaine*; "The Songs Angels Sing"; "Lee-Ah-Loo"; "Miserere" from *Il Trovatore*; "The Lord's Prayer"; "Mama Mia, Che Vo Sape?" and several other selections, in duet with Doretta Morrow or James Whitmore.

Though Mario had been convinced from the outset of the film that there was a dark conspiracy afoot against him, and that, as the successor to Caruso, he should not have been subjected to such a hackneyed role, he insisted on telling Pasternak that he was sorry for all the trouble he had caused him and he hoped they could work more harmoniously in the future. Pasternak was stunned by the turnabout. But he lived on hope, as far as Mario was concerned. All of us who respected his talent and wanted him to be well again lived on hope, too-forlorn as it was.

When the movie was honored with a Command Performance designation before Queen Elizabeth and the English court, Mario's spirits rose again.

"Do you think I've been nothing but a big baby all along?" he asked me one night before we sat down to rehearse.

I looked at him for a moment, trying to frame an honest answer. I knew that if I told him yes, he was just a big baby, it would be an oversimplification, a meaningless answer. I wanted to say to him, "Mario, you are a great talent, perhaps the greatest in your field. But you need a doctor's help. Why don't you get it, now, before it's too late?"

But I could not force the words out.

16. The "Student Prince" Scandal

$\mathscr{I}$N THE nightmare world of Mario there were few people who could be trusted, loved, or respected. But one of them was a delightful little singer and actress named Ann Blyth. From the first time Mario saw Ann he had been drawn to her by her sympathy and understanding for him.

Before that first meeting with Ann, the M-G-M staff had tried to brief Mario on how he should behave in front of this girl. She had been cast to play what Pasternak called Mario's "guardian an- gel" in *The Great Caruso*. Having been fully exposed to Mario's rambunctiousness and longshoreman language, the studio felt there should be a preliminary meeting between Ann and her costar, so that she would see what a perfect gentleman he could be when he tried.

"Please be on your best behavior with Miss Blyth," Pasternak had pleaded with Mario. "She's a fine young lady and will be shocked by any rude words or nasty jokes."

"I'll wash my mouth out with soap," laughed Mario.

Several M-G-M bigwigs had gathered in Pasternak's office for the epochal meeting. Mario showed up first, wearing a tie to show good intent.

"Remember what I said to you, Mario," Pasternak said. "Try your best to be nice."

After Miss Blyth arrived, the talk turned to the forthcoming movie. But everybody seemed to be on edge. There was a formality and stiffness in the air that bothered Mario. He began to fidget. Ann could sense that something was wrong.

Suddenly Mario blurted out, "The hell with this damn nonsense! I'm not acting like Mario Lanza; I'm acting like a jerk."

Pasternak quickly looked at Ann. But Ann wasn't standing where she had been a moment before. She had rushed over to Mario's side and was in the process of giving him a hug.

"I love you, Mario, for being yourself," she said, in a soft voice.

No wonder Mario had great admiration for this girl. No wonder that, when it came time for him to make his next picture, he was beside himself with joy to learn Ann was available to join him again.

That was only one reason for feeling that *The Student Prince*, Pasternak's selection for Mario's next starring vehicle, would be shot without the tempests that rocked *Because You're Mine*. Another was the movie itself: Mario found no fault with Sigmund Romberg's sentimental mittel-Europa operetta; he loved the role of Prince Karl Franz, who thumbs his nose at a proper marriage for the hand of the innkeeper's daughter. And finally, when Mario requested that M-G-M engage my services as his personal musical director, and the studio consented, it appeared that all was serene, that we could expect smooth sailing and a wonderful movie. George Stoll was named as the musical director for the whole film; I was to work closely with him.

Planning sessions were held between Mario, Pasternak, Stoll, director Curtis Bernhardt, Irving Aaronson, the writers, Nicky Brodszky and myself. Mario always seemed in good humor. He told me every day that he anticipated his greatest movie and that his fans would break down the doors to see him in this one.

"If they thought I fractured 'em in *Caruso*, wait'll they see this one," he promised.

I knew he was sincere, but after his distresses of recent weeks I was certain sincerity would not carry him far enough.

Whenever there is singing or dancing in a film, music is pre-recorded before the actual shooting gets under way. When a scene is filmed, the singer then acts out his singing to the sound of the recording, which is played to the scene. This may seem like a complicated and unnecessary process, but there are many good reasons for it. Concentration on obtaining the best possible sound on the sound stage is one of them. The time element is another: a singer may be forced to repeat a selection several times, and it is costly enough to pay large orchestras for this without having a crew of actors on hand waiting for the right "take." So they do the next best thing: they pre-record.

A few hours after the singer has recorded his number on a sound stage, he receives an acetate, which is a recording of the number he has just sung. He then plays the acetate and practices synchronizing his acting with the music. When the actual scene is being shot, a "click-track" is utilized to point out all the appropriate pauses to the singer. Naturally, the pre-recordings are made after all of the dramatic scenes are studied and detailed, so that the singer can give a proper interpretation and expression to each song.

In preparing to make the pre-recordings for *The Student Prince*, Mario and I worked two hours every day for three weeks. Mario was devoted to the task and he didn't touch a drop.

The old, familiar songs by Romberg caught his fancy and were just right for his voice. The nostalgic "Golden Days"; the famous drinking song of the Heidelberg students; the romantic little ballad "Just We Two"; the traditional "Gaudeamus Igitur"; and the warm "Deep in My Heart, Dear," were still the nucleus of the picture's songs. But Nicky Brodszky and lyric writer Paul Francis Webster had added some fine numbers: "Summertime in Heidelberg," "I'll Walk with God," and "Beloved." Mario expressed his satisfaction with them.

When, after our elaborate preparations, we made the actual recordings, an amazing thing occurred. Each of the songs was recorded in just one take! This was not only highly unusual but also seemed to be another good omen.

However, the fireworks began as rehearsals for the movie started.

One day I was present when Mario disagreed violently with director Curt Bernhardt over an interpretation of the Prince Karl part. When Bernhardt had asked for a little less emotion, Mario reacted as though he had been gored.

"How can a great singer take such ridiculous orders?" he shouted for everybody to hear.

From then on Mario complained to me daily about the director, who had become the bane of his existence. He complained in general. He was irked by his pay for the movie: "I'll make them millions, but they don't give a fair share to their biggest star." He was agitated by the actions of an assistant director, whom he accused of having a personal dislike for him. Soon, determined to settle the assistant director once and for all, Mario rushed to Pasternak's office.

"I want that bastard put on another job," screamed Mario.

"I can't fire him for no good reason," replied Pasternak. "He hasn't done anything wrong."

Mario stormed out of the office, enraged anew by Pasternak's rejection. He found Terry Robinson waiting for him outside. Terry took him for a ride in an effort to placate him and reason with him.

"Christ, here I am the big star of this picture, and I can't even get a little favor granted," Mario said.

To Pasternak it was a question of practical strategy: if he acquiesced to Mario once, it would invite dozens of petty, irrational demands. He would lose his authority as the producer of the film. Pasternak says, "This man that Mario wanted me to get rid of was competent as far as I was concerned. He also had a family. What reason could I possibly have for removing him from the picture?"

Perhaps if Joe had known in advance that Mario would take his refusal as an excuse for a walk-out strike, practically without precedent in the motion picture business, he might have pressed for a truce at once.

165

On the first day of shooting, Mario failed to show up for work. When he was finally located, he promised to report the following morning. The following morning, no Mario. And the morning after that, still no Mario.

It went on for days. But as each hour went by, Mario in his seething hostility became more intransigent. They couldn't do this to him, inflict on him some boob of a director who hated him. He would show them.

M-G-M remained adamant. It is questionable whether any other course would have availed them. They were dealing with a man hardly responsible for his actions.

As part of his lamentable, harrowing game of hide-and-seek, Mario was drinking and eating again with the same mad compulsion that characterized all of his periods of emotional crisis. The weight bulged his body into a gross distortion of the man who was supposed to be the romantic lover of *The Student Prince*. Now, even if he wanted to play the role, he couldn't. The self-consciousness over his appearance also returned to haunt his days and nights. Each day he invented new excuses for staying away from the set.

Mario had no income—his salary had been suspended, and M-G-M had invoked a clause in his contract preventing him from working in radio. What was worse, hundreds of workers on the picture—electricians, carpenters, the grips, the property men, the wardrobe and make-up technicians, the sound men—were missing their pay envelopes each week. These, the very people Mario had always prided himself on helping and liking, he was now causing untold hardship. Their losses in pay probably totaled over a half-million dollars.

Several attempts were made to get Mario together with the studio. They all failed. Then, in a clever, last-ditch appeal to Mario as well as the studio, Terry Robinson arranged to bring Tony and Maria Cocozza to meet M-G-M's top executives.

When Maria, Tony and Terry arrived at the studio, they were immediately ushered into the office of Dore Schary, who at this time had succeeded to the head-of-production job at M-G-M. Eddie Mannix, a former amusement park bouncer who had been a favorite of Louis B. Mayer in other years, was on hand. So were Benny Thau, Joe Pasternak and Nick Schenck.

Maria and Tony explained that more than anything in the world they wanted their boy to resume his regular work on the film. Then Terry begged the group to try to understand their troubled star.

"Just how long do you think we can put up with this nonsense?" one of the executives retorted. "It's costing us a great deal of money. You know that, and so does Mario."

"I'm not so sure Mario really does understand," said Terry.

He looked at Maria, her remarkably young and pretty face creased with concern. He had no desire to upset her further, but he felt he had to say it—now, when they were all there.

"This boy," Terry went on, "is my good friend. I want you to know he is badly in need of help. Why doesn't the studio try to help him? We've *all* got to help him!"

Nobody in the room spoke for a few seconds. Then one of the M-G-M brass said, "Mario Lanza is admittedly a top star in this studio. He means a great deal to all of us seated here. But, gentlemen, he is only one man. As much as I may sympathize with him, no one man is bigger than the studio. No one man can disrupt the operation of a studio to this extent. I fail to see what we can do at this time, beyond encouraging him to return to work at once."

It was apparent that the next move was up to Mario.

We all urged him now to make a new try at working himself into shape for the movie. Somehow we reached him and moved him. He decided to go to Palm Springs at once.

Mario rented a $3,000-a-month house there, promised the studio he would return—ready for work—in a few months, and embarked on a brutal diet of one hard-boiled egg, one tomato and one grapefruit each day. Hopeful that Mario could and would keep his word, M-G-M held up production on the picture.

Mario sang each morning at Palm Springs, and his voice was in excellent timbre. As the pounds slowly melted off, I convinced myself that he would fulfill his commitment. Again how wrong, how ridiculously wrong I was!

Mario returned to Hollywood fit as a fiddle. A few days later he went to the office of Dore Schary. An argument ensued. Mario walked out in disgust.

He would never return to do *The Student Prince*. He would never work on it a single day. And two weeks later he couldn't have squeezed into his *Student Prince* costumes even if he wanted to.

On August 22, 1952, M-G-M, furious and frustrated over mounting costs, asked Mario to report the next day for work—or else. He was sent a telegram and was phoned. He did not report.

On September 4, the film was canceled, as far as Mario was concerned.

In late September, a tremendous suit was filed by M-G-M in United States District Court.

The studio charged Mario with breach of contract, asking $695,888 in special damages and $4,500,000 in general damages, which was to cover the prospective losses to M-G-M through the cancellation of the movie. M-G-M also sought an injunction against Mario, restraining him from appearing in concerts, singing on the radio or making any further recordings for the duration of his contract, which was 15 months.

The dispute had become the talk of a town that usually has plenty to gossip about. Said *The New York Times*:

> Whatever the real reasons, Mr. Lanza's hold-out action made him the target of criticism. Interestingly, and indicative of the new awareness of money matters, most of the comment was about the money that the squabble was costing the studio. In the old days of not so long ago, the studio wouldn't get much consideration on that score . . . disciplining a star is one thing, but it is not nearly as important as keeping him on the screen to make money for the stockholders.

It wasn't until May, 1953, that the last was heard at M-G-M about Mario Lanza or the suit. At that time the studio called off its lawsuit in return for the right to use the recordings that Mario had made before the acrimony set in. M-G-M completed *The Student Prince* with Edmund Purdom mouthing the lyrics to Mario's recorded songs. Mario never went to see the picture.

A month prior to that announcement, Mario had been finally discharged from the studio. "It is with extreme regret that M-G-M has been forced to take this action," the handout from Dore Schary said, terminating the turbulent relationship between Mario and his first Hollywood employer.

What had really happened to cause this schism? Had the news Mario received from his accountants and lawyers about the state of his finances actually sapped his will to work and perform? How much had his maniacal dieting done to break down his ability to cope with the realities of the situation? And sick as he was, with his nerves at the breaking point, why wasn't something done about it?

There are no answers to these questions, least of all easy ones. But it has always struck me as rather strange that so little effort was made to save this man from himself. The whole town moved in the name of money, and the victim was a simple, terrified soul named Mario.

17. The Blackest Years

*F*ROM this point on, it was all downhill for Mario.

In the next three and a half years he barely existed, eating and drinking and raging in his Bel-Air home. He preferred isolation from everybody and everything. For the most part, nobody saw him but Betty, Terry, his parents, and myself. And what made it even worse was that few, even those who once received his gifts or his favors or his approval, expressed any interest in seeing him or in breaking through his self-imposed exile.

He had become a forgotten man years before his time—years before his career might have been expected to reach its peak.

"This is miserable, isn't it?" he said to me one day when I came to visit him and play for him to relax his tormented mind and body.

It was. He punished himself as only the true masochist can.

Sometimes there would be a caller. Hedda Hopper, the columnist who had been so helpful and admiring at the outset of Mario's career, presented herself one day.

"I'd like to speak to Mario," she said to me.

The previous night, Mario had thrown a frightening fit after a long morning and afternoon with the bottle, and he had given strict orders that he didn't want to see anybody.

"I'm sorry," I said to Hedda. "He isn't feeling well. His throat and his chest are hurting him. He really isn't in shape to see anyone."

But Mario came out and visited with her for a few minutes. Then he excused himself, leaving me to "explain" as much as I could to Hedda.

I tried to get him interested in philosophy, the early Greeks. I wanted him to take his mind off his troubles, whatever they were. I brought him books to read. Sometimes he tried to read the books; sometimes he'd listen to me discuss the Greeks. But more often he was a mass of exposed nerve ends. A child's laughter or an auto horn would throw him into a tirade; the failure of the cook to produce a properly seasoned Italian dish would ignite an unforgettable scene of frenzy.

I was on a retainer to keep coaching him. But he wasn't singing each day, as he should have been. Often when I came he'd be asleep. I would wait for hours, through the middle of a day, but he still slept on, bathed in sweat from the beer, the champagne and the wine he drank constantly, over the angry objections of Betty.

When he was awake, and reasonably fit to talk to, I lectured him on what he was doing to himself.

"Don't you see that you're ruining your whole life?" I said.

Mario would only stare at me, petulant and outraged. "Nobody understands me," he'd say.

He found a thousand excuses to justify himself for what he was doing. One day it was M-G-M that was to blame for everything, the next it was a director, the next an assistant director, the next it was Betty. Everyone was trying to destroy him, to ruin the greatest gift to the musical world since Caruso.

All of us tried to fight his growing addiction to alcohol. Betty informed the three servants in the house that she would fire any one of them she saw supplying beer or wine to Mario. But he managed to get it anyway. He would sneak it into the kitchen late at night, having it brought in from the outside. He would hide it in the bathroom. Some days he drank beer all day, by himself. Then when night came, he'd switch to champagne. If he temporarily stayed off beer or champagne, it would simply mean he had substituted wine. "This is the best," he'd say. "That hard stuff hurts the throat." And when beer, wine, and champagne got boring, he'd embark on a liqueur kick.

All the while he was eating like Gargantua. He went to 230, then 240, then 250 pounds. The mention of exorcise made him laugh. He refused in those early months even to walk around the house.

I considered it a major triumph to get him to go for a ride in his big white Cadillac. So did Terry—until he got the fright of his life.

For days Mario had been sitting in his room glowering at the floor, moodily listening to records.

"Let's get some fresh air, Tiger," Terry urged.

Finally Mario agreed but insisted on driving. That was perfectly all right with Terry. Anything to get Mario out of the house.

As he drove along, Mario was oblivious of the magnificent California countryside, the wonderful aroma of the thousands of oranges, the sweet gallimaufry of flowers on the side of the road.

Terry tried to break Mario out of his black mood. "Think of it," he said cheerily. "If you stopped this car right now and stepped out, you'd be mobbed by your fans. People would stop their cars. They'd recognize you and want to talk to you and touch you. But if I got out, hell, they'd run right over me."

Mario never took his eyes off the road. "I don't give a damn for all of it," he said at last. "What is it all worth? What's it all mean?" Then he slowly ran his left hand across his brow. "I've already lived a million years in my head," he said. "I've had enough of it."

Tears began running down Mario's cheek.

The big Cadillac was now thundering along Coldwater Canyon, a tortuous, precipitous roadway, at 80 miles an hour. Mario's eyes took on a glazed, unseeing stare; his hands gripped the wheel in a vise.

Then the speedometer showed 90 miles an hour. A slight mistake, a swerve to the right by even a few inches, could send this desperate driver and his companion to their deaths far below.

Terry didn't dare grab the wheel away from Mario. Nor did he dare to joke or plead with Mario to slow down. He was speechless, frozen by fear.

Breathlessly, Mario began to speak. "Wouldn't it be great if we could ride right off this highway! Off the side of the mountain and into wild flames!"

He was being very melodramatic, Terry knew. But Terry could also see that they were now doing 100 miles an hour, and the night was beginning to descend on them.

"Think of it, Terry," Mario continued, his voice pitched to a high shout above the roar of the motor. "Every goddam newspaper in the country would have headlines tomorrow—*Mario Lanza and Best Friend Die in Flaming Auto Wreck!* That's the way to go. . . ."

Terry didn't doubt Mario's suicidal intentions. But it was also suicidal to try to stop him. So he shrank down in the front seat, waiting, prepared for the moment when the car would propel itself into space. If he was lucky, he would live through it. Poor Mario, he was really crazy, and he was going to finish the two of them. . . .

The car went faster and still faster.

Then, with a great lurch, it began shrieking to a grinding halt.

In the sudden silence Terry heard himself panting like a winded animal. Mario's face was bathed in sweat as if someone dumped a pail over his head; his eyes were bulging out of his head. Terry reached over and clutched his arm.

"What made you stop?" he said, in a low voice. "I thought you were going to kill us both."

"I would have," said Mario. "I don't know what stopped me. We're both lucky to be alive."

It began to get chilly then, and Terry changed places with Mario behind the wheel and drove the rest of the way. "

Neither of them spoke again till they got home.

When George London came to visit, Mario's condition was a great shock to him. George had seen Mario infrequently since the Bel Canto days—and then things did not always go too well between them. But he had read of Mario's inactivity, and was anxious to help his old friend if he could.

Mario was happy to see George. The two spent a day talking and walking. They stayed close to the house though, for Mario didn't want to be seen or recognized.

"He was drunk that day," recalls George, "but full of remorse, and almost peaceful in his manner. 'You're my only friend,' he kept saying. Then he hugged me, like a child will hug a father or mother or someone he deeply loves. I was touched, but terribly disturbed to see him like this."

Several years later, when Mario was living out the last months of his life, he would listen endlessly to George's records, repeating how happy he was that George had achieved such success in opera. It was the thing that Mario always secretly envied, because he wanted recognition as a true artist more than anything else in the world.

Only people like George London or Rocky Marciano, the heavyweight champion of the world, were truly welcome at Mario's home. Terry had introduced Marciano to Mario and the two got along well together. Mario had always been a frustrated prize fighter and, at a time when he was in better spirits, he had built himself a $3,000 ring in his back yard. Mario and Terry went at it with the skill of professionals.

Mario developed a great feeling of loyalty to Rocky. One night the late Max Baer, a former heavyweight champion of the world during the 1930's and reputed to hit as hard as any fighter that ever lived, came to see Mario.

"Any friend of Rocky's is a friend of mine," said Mario.

During the course of the evening, as Max monopolized the conversation, the subject of Marciano's ability came up. Max disparaged Rocky's talents, insisting that he could have thrashed Rocky if they had fought during his heyday.

"I'll use Rocky's style," said Mario, "and you show me how you would have licked him."

So Mario and Max, two notorious high livers and conspicuously out of shape, squared off in the living room and started to bob and weave. Then Max threw a right hand. As Mario blocked the punch he shot over a ringing left hook that caught Max completely by surprise and landed him on a nearby sofa. Mario was delighted with himself.

But such moments of happiness were all too brief. The next day he was back doing the same self-destructive things as before, hurting himself irreparably and hurting others in the process.

He had violent fits when he drank, and once, in the grip of the DT's, he almost crushed Terry's hand as Terry struggled to calm him. Mario had enormous strength in his body, even though he neglected it. When he lost control of his reason he became a wild man. Some of his employees had stopped working for him because they feared they would be physically harmed.

Within two years Mario had practically wrecked two entire houses that he rented, and he was sued for damages totaling over $50,000.

We tried to encourage him to join a chapter of Alcoholics Anonymous that had many Hollywood celebrities as active and interested members. But he steadfastly refused.

"I can take care of myself," he'd say sullenly.

Then, in a moment of naked" exposure, he would sit weeping violently and crashing his fists against his knees. "Why can't I stop drinking?" he would cry. "Why? Why? I hate the stuff. What am I doing to myself?"

None of us knew.

These may have been the "lost years" for Mario. But the outside world hadn't forgotten him. Offers kept coming in for concert engagements, radio and TV performances, public appearances and projected movies. But Mario remained immobilized, chained by compulsions that were incomprehensible to those of us around him.

One night, with Lloyd Shearer and Terry, Mario went across the border to Tiajuana, Mexico. To make certain that he wouldn't be recognized, Mario wore dark glasses, a felt hat pulled low, and a coat collar shielding the lower part of his bloated features.

They walked unnoticed into a little bar. After a few glasses of beer, Mario started to sing. All talk and activity ceased, the Mexicans gathered around his table, listening intently to the impromptu songfest.

Here he was, out of work, no pay coming in, up to his neck in debts and bills and troubles, singing for absolutely nothing. That night those attentive Mexicans were the most appreciative audience in the world. They were listening to a man willing to sing for them for nothing, when he could have made in one engagement more money than any of them had seen in their lives.

Strangely, as the man went to ruin his voice did not. It was still truthfully prodigious. Alan Kayes, the manager of RCA Victor's Red Seal Artists and Repertoire, once commented: "Mario's voice may have lacked the proper diction, and he may have been undisciplined, and lacking in taste and musicality. But it could never be said that his voice was deteriorating, too. Not at all. If anything, in the last years of his life Mario's voice became richer and darker."

For a few weeks I tried to pique Mario's interest in stamps. I have always collected all sorts of stamps, and I thought this might be good therapy for him.

"FDR collected stamps," I told him. I explained that some stamps originally worth two and three cents increased in value to $10, $15, and more. For a while he seemed to be fascinated, and gave me $150 at a time to purchase new sheets of stamps at the post office.

After Mario had invested almost $1,000 in his new hobby, one of his business managers discouraged him from continuing. "It's only an unnecessary expense," he told Mario.

In 1953 I was appointed musical director of the Highland Park Symphony Orchestra, near Los Angeles. In my first concert a young lyric soprano named Marcella Reale sang my song, "You Are My Love," and dedicated it to the Cocozzas, who were present.

When Maria and Tony saw Mario the next day they told him about the song, and how warmly and gloriously it had been delivered by Marcella.

"You must record it, Mario," they said.

"I promised Costa a long time ago to do it and I never have," said Mario. "I'll do it now, and nobody's going to stop me."

When I heard of Mario's decision, I was delighted. He hadn't shown such desire or conviction in many months.

But twenty-four hours later, when I dropped by to see how he was feeling, he told me that Betty didn't think the song was good for him and that RCA agreed with this opinion.

I had been waiting for over two years for him to record it and now he was backing down again. He could see that I was hurt and upset.

The next day Mario called me. "I don't give a damn what anybody thinks," he assured me. "We're going to record it!"

So finally Mario and I recorded "You Are My Love," along with three other numbers, at Republic Studios. The disc jockeys were kind to it, and so was the public. It was a mild hit, and Mario was pleased that he had done it.

"I'm sorry we didn't do it a long time ago," he said.

In December, 1953, when *The Student Prince* was about to be released (without Mario in the starring role, of course), Mario asked me to return to Hollywood to work with him on a *Student Prince* album for RCA.

Was the long night really over for Mario? Was he actually ready to start work again? These were the questions that came to my mind as I boarded my plane for California.

It wasn't long before I had my answers. On the day of the first recording session, while Mario was warming up his voice, I noticed he had been drinking. Nothing had changed, I thought to myself. I had made the trip for nothing.

I stopped the rehearsal.

"Why are you doing this again?" I cried.

"It's just to warm up my voice, to clear my throat," Mario answered. "Don't worry about it."

I knew another failure was due. I wanted to pick up my things then and there and leave the Warner Brothers recording stage. But even if Mario was going to let us down, I couldn't let him down. I would try to go through with it, as much as it hurt.

We began to record. His singing was faulty and bad. I couldn't begin to compare it with any of Mario's past efforts or the original soundtrack he had made for M-G-M. We had to put aside "When It's Summertime in Heidelberg," because Mario could not summon up the sweetness of quality I demanded on the number. As we launched into another selection Mario's chauffeur arrived with a package. I didn't have to ask questions about it. It was several cans of beer.

I stopped the session immediately. "We can't work under these conditions," I said to Mario.

"I don't give a damn," he said. And he lurched out, leaving us without a single decent recording for an entire day's work.

Before the next session, which was scheduled two days later, I begged Mario to look at what he was doing. I made the plea as a friend interested in his welfare and in the welfare of his family. "I'm not a minister," I said, "but I'll have to talk to you like one. Please stop this drinking. It's killing you!"

I had tried. But without success.

181

At the second session Mario's breath control, usually fabulous, failed him. Phlegm was agitating his throat and his tones were distressingly poor. We called it quits at the end of the day and completely canceled out the third session we had planned.

Mario's depression was deeper than ever now. In the past it was never his voice that failed, only determination. Now his capacity to perform had been found wanting. I had no alternative but to notify him I was going to return to New York.

However, just before I left an idea occurred to me. I suggested to Mario that I would do research in New York in an effort to find some arias from little-known operas. I would present these to Mario and if he liked any of them he could, if he so desired, bring them to the attention of the public.

"There are moments of magnificent achievement, even in operas that have failed dismally," I told him. "Maybe you would like to concentrate on such music."

When the idea seemed to appeal to him, I returned to New York and did my research in the public libraries and in the private library of the Broude brothers, the music publishers.

The Broude brothers—Irving and Alexander—gave me fifteen complete vocal scores of rare operas. All told I accumulated about thirty-five tenor arias for Mario. It was just a long-shot chance. But maybe it would work. Maybe this would mean something to Mario—a challenge, a completely new experience.

When I returned to Hollywood at the end of February, 1954, I immediately rushed to see him. I told him what I had collected and he asked me to play them for him.

I sat down at the piano in his big music room, full of its records, books, magazines and pictures. Across from me was Mario, slumped down on the couch. I played continuously for several hours.

By now Mario's face was lit up, and he told me of his desire to work on these arias.

"Do you really want to?" I asked.

"Yes," he said. "This is exciting music, Costa."

How many times had I believed Mario, and then he had failed me or reneged on a promise or a plan? I couldn't possibly count it on my fingers. But I was a glutton for punishment. I would try again with him.

We began to work together once more. Each morning I would come to the house, and we practiced these arias from 10 to 12. Mario was heavy and sluggish, but his attitude was cooperative. And his drinking seemed to have diminished.

Nicky Brodszky dropped by one day to listen to Mario.

"I think Mario is singing well again," he confided to me. "I hope he has this thing licked."

Mario's spirits were lighter than they had been in months; the desire to be left alone was yielding to the old need for people around him, no matter who they might be. He was so stimulated by the old operas that sometimes he would call me in the early hours of the morning.

"Costa, you must come over right now. I want to sing," he'd say.

If this was a release for his frustrations, I was willing to help him as much as I could.

But now that friends were finding their way back to Mario's house, it was difficult to restrain him from engaging in drinking bouts at these parties. Betty and I warned him repeatedly. But it was always the same response—"Oh, just one more little one. It won't hurt."

One night, while a party progressed at Mario's, he became enamored of his power and emotions. Singing at the top of his mighty lungs, his voice echoed in the night.

I shook with anger. "You're destroying your voice," I said. "I won't play another note for you."

When he insisted and cajoled, I became disgusted and stalked out of the house.

The next day Mario refused to see me. And when the end of the week came, and I was supposed to be paid by his business manager, no check was forthcoming. I stopped calling him and made up my mind not to visit him.

It went on like this for three weeks. Then one morning Mario phoned.

"What the hell is the matter with you, you temperamental Greek?" he shouted. "Why don't you get over here and rehearse these arias with me? I love them."

"Are you sure you want to see me?" I asked.

"Of course," he said. "Forgive me. I've got a lot on my mind."

When I arrived at the house, he presented me with my back pay. We started working again.

I had always noticed that after each upset with Mario, after each disagreement and tempest, his warmth toward me increased.

Invariably it was a repentant Mario who begged me to understand and come back. And it was always a drinking orgy that would set him off again on the same bleak, hopeless trail to nowhere.

One day, as we were going over one of Leoncavallo's lesser-known operas, Mario asked me to stop playing. "Costa," he said, "I want you to know that I'm dead broke. I can't pay you any more—not even a dime. I'm going crazy trying to pay my bills."

I had long suspected the financial hardships that had befallen him. I was willing, now that he discussed it in such frank terms, to express my devotion to him.

"I'll work with you for nothing," I told him.

I know he was deeply touched. But he didn't utter a word. Instead, he started to cry.

I walked out of the music room, leaving him alone with his thoughts.

18. The First "Comeback"

FOR many weeks CBS, in a typical demonstration of vice-presidential tenacity, had been trying to invade Mario's sanctuary, to lure him into circulation with an offer of $40,000.

Their plan was to reintroduce him to the public on a Thursday night color television spectacular called the *Shower of Stars*. To the CBS brass it was a simple matter: Mario could perform any way he wanted—by the accepted method of synchronizing his lips with recordings of his voice, or by actually singing his numbers before the vast television audience.

To Mario singing "live" was a frightening assignment. "How do I know if my voice will be any good that night?" he asked. The chance of a breakdown before so many leering faces and taunting eyes prompted him to take the easy way out.

Mario chose to "sing" to his own recordings—two of which, "Vesti la giubba" and "Marechiare," had been recorded several years before, when he had been in peak condition. The whole show, including Betty Grable's selections, was pre-recorded.

For two weeks before the show, Mario and I worked over two hours each day on the synchronization of his mouth movements with his own recordings. Then, on the night of the show itself, I was there to steer Mario through his expensive engagement. I stood behind the camera and, while Mario watched me like a hungry hawk, we "attacked" (started) and "released" (stopped) as best we could.

Mario never anticipated the furor that would be raised, nor the ugly remarks that would be recorded in the press. Had he chosen to sing several easy rhythm songs, such as the ones that were selected for use by Miss Grable, he would have had little difficulty with the synchronization. He might even have escaped the notice of the sharp-eyed critics.

As it turned out, Mario was hardly an expert at mouthing lyrics to the old records. We tried our best to master the technique but we failed. That was Mario's misfortune, and the viewers screamed and the papers exposed the "fraud"—a harsh word for such an innocuous practice.

Jack Gould, the TV critic of *The New York Times*, expressed his personal outrage by calling Mario's performance "Zombie TV." Caption writers were distraught: "Mario showed up. But did his voice?" The whole thing was "obvious" to Hollywood columnist Sheilah Graham.

With accusations filling the air, CBS heatedly denied that Mario had mouthed the lyrics to a background of old recordings. Then, fuming with professional pride, Mario entered the fray, saying indignantly that he did not have to fake anything with his voice. "I can still out-sing anyone in the world," he exploded. "I made those recordings a few days before."

If Mario had chosen to tell the truth at the start of the furor, he might have immediately halted the flood of inspired literature on the subject. But, refusing to listen to advice, he hit out at his tormentors and detractors. In the process, he employed the worst weapon of all—lies.

Now the heat was too great for CBS. Making an effort to clear up the controversy once and for all, CBS President J. L. Volkenburg issued a statement pointing out that CBS felt it was better to present Mario this way, rather than to forego his appearance entirely. He added that Mario's doctor had warned it would be impossible for him to sing.

The statement, of course, was not completely fair to Mario. As usual he was afraid; he was weak from dieting; he was in the midst of a crisis over his TV debut. But he could have sung that night in spite of all. CBS should have made that clear. They didn't.

It then remained for Mario himself to accept the challenge. "They're all laughing at me," he said. "They don't think I still have a great voice. I'll have to show them."

Within forty-eight hours of CBS's official explanation, Mario made up his mind to hold a private concert for some of the doubting Thomases of the press. He asked Maestro Giacomo Spadone, once a coach of Caruso, to act as his accompanist on this day of his trial. The maestro accepted gladly.

The ladies and gentlemen of the Hollywood press flocked to Mario's Bel-Air house. Many of them, I'm sure, sensed a disaster, felt confident that they would hear a mockery of the voice that Mario once possessed. Louella Parsons, Hedda Hopper, Erskine Johnson, Bob Thomas, Sheilah Graham, Jimmy Bacon—they all came. Altogether the attendance was about forty.

Mario greeted them all amiably, though he had nothing but hatred for many of them. If only he could have talked to them sensibly, he might have been able to win them over. But he couldn't. What he could still do, as he would prove in only a few seconds, was sing. And sing better than any of these reporters, columnists, soothsayers and essayists had ever heard anyone sing!

With his collar open and his belt buckle loosened, Mario gave them what they came for—proof that the gift of nature hadn't yet deserted him, despite everything that had transpired.

When he had finished singing "Be My Love" and selections from *Pagliacici* and *La Bohéme*, the writers cheered him to the echo. There was no doubt in their minds now that Mario was the victim of his own poor judgment.

In the next few months, Mario again slipped into obscurity. He felt he had proven his point—didn't he have the greatest voice in the world?—and so there was no need for him to extend himself any further for the ingrates. He sought his solace in food and drink; they were companions that would demand nothing of him. Later, they would extract their price—his health.

The state of Mario's finances was desperate these days. He was fond of telling me, this man who had made a fortune in one year alone, that "I've gone from nothing to millions and back again." The extent of his bitterness was indescribable. But he was willing to do next to nothing about it, until he happened to make the acquaintance of Al Teitelbaum, a well-known Hollywood furrier who made a practice of lending his wares to some of the town's fashionable actresses for publicity purposes.

Terry Robinson, at Betty's request, had taken one of her fur coats in to Teitelbaum's store. She was eager to receive some money for it and had heard of Teitelbaum's generosity.

Teitelbaum was shocked to learn of Mario's bankrupt state. "Are they that broke?" he asked Terry.

"Things are pretty bad for them," admitted Terry. "I've been trying to help. But I don't have much."

The furrier then drove out to see Mario. After a brief discussion, Teitelbaum decided to give Mario $60,000, to help pay off his large debts and living expenses. In exchange, Teitelbaum became Mario's personal manager.

Now, under Teitelbaum's prodding, Mario would try another "comeback." It sounded too good to be true. Teitelbaum was convinced it was the beginning of better times for Mario. There was much that Teitelbaum did not understand about Mario, past and present, but he was acting out of a desire to help the man, and for that he can scarcely be criticized.

Teitelbaum booked Mario into a two-week stand at the New Frontier Hotel in Las Vegas. The engagement was worth $50,000 a week. Not even the Mario Lanza of 1951 could laugh off that kind of money.

But now came the dieting and training again. The whole family, along with two nurses, Terry, and Ray Sinatra, went to Palm Springs, Mario's training ground of other days. A magnificent home, with swimming pool and tennis court, was rented for $8,000 a month. The grueling hikes, exhausting exercises, and stringent diet gradually melted Mario down from 260 pounds. It seemed as though he was perennially on the treadmill, but there was no way out save the $100,000 beckoning him in Las Vegas.

Four days before Mario was scheduled to make his night club debut at the New Frontier, the Lanzas descended in full force on the town. Sam Lewis, the manager of the hotel, had arranged to fly in over 1,000 of the press for the opening. The town, never noticeably allergic to press-agented agitation, was full of gamblers and smart money men who knew all about the Lanza defections and were betting large sums that Mario would never show up for the opening night.

These operators won their money.

It had been over a hundred degrees in the Palm Springs desert. So when the Lanza entourage hit Las Vegas, that April day in 1955, they expected more of the same. But it was chilly in Vegas, and a couple of days before opening night Mario insisted his throat felt sore and raw. Terry went downstairs to a drugstore and bought some medicine.

On the morning of the show, after testing his voice, Mario announced to Betty that he thought he had a sore throat.

"You always do this," she said angrily. "There's nothing the matter with you!"

Betty's retort, coming when Mario needed reassurances and not the truth, threw him into a frenzy. He swung at his terrified wife, seized any object within reach of his hands, kicked over the furniture, ripped at the bedspreads, smashed out the bulbs.

When the wild melee ended, Mario was physically and emotionally exhausted. It was inconceivable that he could go on that night. The gamblers had already won their bets.

But the effort had to be made.

White-faced and shaking, Mario struggled to get a grip on himself. But his nerves were shot: they needed to be soothed, not forced. His mind was in turmoil: it needed rest, not driving to recall lyrics. Panicked, desolate, Mario fought fitfully against the terror that threatened to grind his life, and the life of his wife, into an unspeakable horror.

Someone in town—a "friend"—knew exactly what it was that Mario needed to obtain quick release from his anguish. He knew where it could be obtained at once. He got it. And he let Mario have it, and it wasn't liquor.

Then Mario, reeling and inarticulate, went to see Ben Hecht, the writer, who was stopping at the Sands Hotel.

They drank champagne together for hours. It was a way to forget it, to linger in another world. Now Mario was languid and tired. Now he could sleep, relax, and forget what he was supposed to be doing in the New Frontier that night.

At last Mario had stopped battling his other mortal enemies and his private demons. He was asleep, a fitful sleep—but one that would transplant him to other places, certainly sweeter and less demanding than a night club floor and a $100,000 obligation. This was the peace Mario had sought.

But backstage at the New Frontier there was no peace. At the last minute, when it became apparent that Mario was thoroughly incapable of fulfilling his date, Jimmy Durante was pressed into service. So were dancer Ray Bolger and singer Mindy Carson.

That kind and genial man Schnozzola did what he could to cover up for this boy, to explain away what had befallen him.

"Believe me, folks," Durante said to the crowd of over 500 that packed the New Frontier's Venus Room, "Mario's a very sick boy. They have him in an oxygen tent, and he's unconscious."

The aftermath added sensation to sensation. The hotel management was in a blind fury about the cancellation. Though it was officially announced at the time that Mario was suffering from upper respiratory infections and laryngitis, and though the medicine that Terry had picked up was pointed to as corroboration, few were inclined to believe it. The hotel claimed that it had to pick up a tab of $20,000 for those first-nighters and optimists who had come to hear Mario in his debut, and threats of giant lawsuits filled the air.

The columnists were in no mood to forgive and forget. Hedda Hopper's grapevine had it that "Mario was well enough in the afternoon" when he visited Ben Hecht; and Miss Parsons, perhaps coming closer to the truth, wrote: "He suffers from an overwhelming, clutching terror that he may get up to sing and nothing will come out."

The worst indignity of all befell the entire Lanza family a few days later—the New Frontier management invited all of them to leave the premises at once. It was a wretched end to a chapter that had started out so hopefully.

To make matters worse, Al Teitelbaum was also in hot water now. And Mario, although an innocent bystander in Al's trouble, won his usual share of newspaper space.

One night Mario drove into town to visit Teitelbaum at his store. Getting no response at the back door, Mario went around to the front of the store. Teitelbaum and his fur cutter admitted him.

Teitelbaum then showed Mario adhesive tape marks on his clothing and his hands. "I've just been robbed," he told Mario. "They've taken everything off my fur racks and out of my vault."

Mario, in approaching the store, had seen no bandits, no getaway truck.

Teitelbaum checked his depleted stock, found that 231 furs worth $248,000 were missing, and made a claim. But the police disbelieved his story. After an investigation by the Beverly Hills Police Department, two ex-convicts admitted that they had been hired by Teitelbaum to stage a fake robbery for insurance money. Teitelbaum, the man who had eagerly helped Mario, was convicted and received a one-year jail sentence.

19. Licia Albanese

$\mathcal{F}$OR Mario, who seemed to attract trouble at every turn, there now came a long overdue—if brief—change in fortune.

Many years before, Eddie O'Brien had suggested to both Mario and Warner Brothers that James M. Cain's novel *Serenade* would make an excellent vehicle for a Lanza movie. Now, with Mario's contractual obligations to M-G-M at an end, Warner Brothers decided to act on Eddie's advice and cast him as the poor boy who falls in love with a rich but feckless woman. Joan Fontaine was to play the woman who at first supported the youth as he trained to become a great singer, then deserted him for a sculptor on the night of his Metropolitan Opera debut.

But there was another woman in the movie. And it was she who became one of Mario's last true friends, perhaps his most understanding and sympathetic friend. She was Licia Albanese, a raven-haired lyric soprano of Italian birth who for over two decades had maintained her position as one of the truly great performers of the Metropolitan Opera.

In the eighteen days that Licia Albanese spent in Hollywood working on *Serenade* with Mario (she appeared as Desdemona in a sequence from *Otello*) she won his undying respect and admiration. And she started with a big handicap, for Mario automatically disliked most "long-hairs" of the opera, the artists he thought he had to show up—beat at their own game.

But with Licia it was different. From the first meeting Mario had with Licia a deep feeling of trust and mutual confidence grew between them. Licia had heard all of the stories that circulated about Mario. She knew some were true. She also knew many were false. She knew others were downright malicious.

But she was not a woman to prejudge others. She would make up her own mind about Mario as an artist and as a man.

It didn't take her long to form an opinion of Mario, the singer. After she listened to him sing a few times, and after they sang a duet together, she said, "This boy has, to me, a greater voice than Caruso. He has the greatest voice I have ever heard."

One night, after the work for the day was at an end, Mario came to Licia's dressing room. "I'd like to talk to you," he said.

"Talk all night if you like, Mario," she said.

Already Licia had sensed how troubled Mario was. And now, she thought, if she could help by being a good listener, she would be only too willing to try.

"Everyone says I'm a bad boy," began Mario, almost shyly. "Do you think I am a bad boy?"

"You're not a bad boy," Licia said, looking squarely into his eyes, which had misted over with tears. "You're just ten boys in one."

"But I *am* bad," he insisted. "Do you want to know some of the things I have done?"

"I don't care about them," she said. "Even saints are not perfect, my dear. Why don't you read about the beloved St. Francis of Assisi, and you will find out that he, too, might have done some bad things?"

Long ago Mario had rejected his religion. He had refused to accept it in much the same way he refused to accept psychiatry, or the help of his friends. Licia was the first person in years whom he suffered to bring up the subject.

Mario talked about himself for several hours, and Licia patiently listened. A good deal of the time, Mario cried.

"I think you owe it to yourself to see a doctor, Mario," Licia said.

"You be my doctor," said Mario.

As the days went by, and as the filming progressed smoothly, much of the credit for keeping Mario at peace belonged to Licia.

When she heard sneering remarks uttered about him by extras or stagehands, she immediately rallied to his defense.

"He thinks he's better than Caruso," they'd say.

And Licia would retort, "He is."

And Mario would tell anybody that wanted to listen that Licia Albanese was "the greatest, a singer right from the toes up."

"I love her," he said feelingly.

When Licia's associates on the movie sought to find out why it was that Mario acted so "differently," so "gently" around her, she refused to concede that she had any special charm or held the answers to the riddle of his behavior.

"It is not that he's any different around me," she would tell them. "It's only that he is a boy who needs continual reassurance and affection. In Hollywood he has found few people who can give him this, or who want to."

But now that she knew and thought she understood Mario, Licia was grieved by him. "I felt he was a terribly sick boy, tortured by a lack of true understanding," she says, "and every day after I left him, I prayed for him."

She was not blind to the fact that if his deportment in her presence was commendable, he was still drinking. She tried to fight this battle for Mario, too—in her own way.

"After we sang a duet one day," she recalls, "I asked Mario if he wanted to celebrate by having a glass of wine with me? This would be better, I thought, than the way he was doing it."

And on those not infrequent occasions when Mario returned from a short absence, she'd ask him where he had been.

"Just to the bathroom," Mario would reply.

"Oh, Mario, you are telling me fibs," she'd say. "You went to get a drink. I don't want you spoiling your beautiful voice."

"Please don't get mad at me."

"I'd never be mad at you, Mario," Licia would say soothingly, "I love your voice."

One afternoon, after Mario had just completed a thrilling rendition of Schubert's "Ave Maria," Licia was quick to notice a strange look that came over his' face as he walked to his dressing room. His eyes were popping out of head, and he seemed to be staring into an abyss of loneliness and desperation.

"Don't you feel well, Mario?" Licia asked him.

He stopped at the door of his room and slowly began to wipe the moisture off his face with a towel. She saw that his hands were trembling, that his lips moved without words forming.

Then she heard him say: "I'm going to have a short life. You'll see. I'm going to die young, maybe tomorrow or the next day."

"You will be all right," she said. "Don't keep worrying about yourself. God bless you."

When Licia left Hollywood, after her role in *Serenade* was completed, she was happy to be leaving: this verdant land of plenty was not for her. But she was sorry to bid Mario good-by. She knew he could use her support, her tolerance, her understanding. But she came back to New York, to the Metropolitan Opera where she rightfully belonged, and where, perhaps, Mario belonged too, had the fates been kinder to him.

She cherishes those few days when she got to know Mario. "He always sang with his heart on his lips," she says. "The world cannot forget such a great singer."

Mario's efforts in his first movie since *Because You're Mine* were generally hailed by the critics.

"After some three years away from pictures," noted *Variety*, "Mario Lanza returns in better voice than ever . . . a robust, soaring tenor . . . many will find Schubert's 'Ave Maria' a tremendously moving experience as Lanza sings it in an old San Felipe, Mexico, church to the accompaniment of an organ."

The news magazines commented on the seventeen songs and operatic arias that he sang. But they did not leave untouched the grim realities.

"At singing weight of 240, he looks like a colossal ravioli set on toothpicks," wrote Time's move critic. "His face, aflame from rich living, has the appearance of a giant red pepper."

Then both *Time* and *Newsweek* came to the crux of the matter. After the isolation, how good was Mario Lanza's voice? Was it now a burned-out remnant of the real Lanza? Had it grown rusty, tired or obsolete during the period of fractional self-destruction?

"The big voice is as big as ever," reported *Time.*

"Mario Lanza is still in possession of that God-given high C," said *Newsweek.*

Roger Brown, writing in the September 29, 1956 issue of *Saturday Review*, summed up the hopes of many:

> The voice of Mario Lanza yearns toward the operatic stage, and I dare predict it will carry him there. The great singer who played Caruso has begun to look like and to act like Italian tenors everywhere . . . he cocks his ear to savor a pianissimo, trembles with the beauty of his own tone. While he sings he molds the melodic line with his hands. He postures, overacts, strains, displays an immodest infatuation with his voice. . . .

These were, the writer insisted, unmistakably the marks of a man who could no longer serve a Hollywood where underplaying had become the style and the rule.

The combination of a fine tenor voice, a youthful handsome appearance and friendly, unassuming American manners, Brown thought, had produced the "greatest film success ever attained by a singer of operatic quality."

But now Brown could see Mario ready, physically and emotionally, for the great challenge of opera.

They were words of insight and vision, but the dark workings of Mario's mind could never be analyzed or predicted.

20. *"Seven Hills of Rome"*

$\mathscr{M}$ARIO had always longed to see Italy, the birthplace of his greatest hero, Caruso. So in May, 1957, he set out for Rome with his entire family. He thought that his mere presence in this wonderful city might rejuvenate him. We thought, hopefully, that he would make up his mind here to devote his talents to the opera, his true love.

But even in Rome there was the question of money, and though he had been existing to pay his debts, Mario refused to scale down his standard of living. He still conceived of himself as a singing potentate who was obliged to entertain lavishly and lustily. His villa—its living room, said columnist Hy Gardner, was "slightly larger than a jai alai *fronton*"—became the stop-off point for visiting firemen. Almost anybody in town could wangle an invitation to Mario's for an unforgettable feast. Of course, Mario paid all the bills.

Mario's villa rented for $1,000 a month, very expensive for Rome, and was located at 56 Brussels in a neighborhood called Savoia, which was once the home and grounds of the royal family. It was built of heavy white stone and a light brown brick, surrounded by a high stone fence, tall parasol pines and cypresses. A five-story building, it had originally been built by the late dictator Benito Mussolini and was presented to Field Marshal Badoglio in gratitude for his leadership in the war against the Ethiopians.

Mario rented the bottom floor only, but the fifteen rooms were ample for himself and Betty, the four children, a half-dozen servants, a cat, two dogs, and several canaries. Next to a giant dining room that featured a table seating twenty, there was a large music room with a study. Well furnished, richly draped and carpeted, the house still managed to look empty. When Mario sang in the music room, his voice echoed through the rooms and could be heard clearly on the enormous patio.

This was where Mario took up his last stand against his fate. This was the villa where his final orgies were staged, his final battles fought.

To pay for it all, Mario looked for movie work and found it in *Seven Hills of Rome*. The film was to be produced by LeCloud-Titanus, financed and distributed by Mario's old bosses, M-G-M. Mario was to receive $50,000 at the start of production and a balance of $100,000 on completion of the picture. *Seven Hills of Rome* was budgeted at about a million dollars.

Maurice "Red" Silverstein, a vice-president and International and Eastern Production Head of M-G-M, was assigned as trouble shooter to protect the studio's interests.

Silverstein was a fortunate choice. Leaving other work behind him in New York, he seldom let Mario out of sight. He lunched with him every day, saw him frequently in the evenings. He tried his best to keep Mario on an even keel, to prevent him from lapsing into bouts of eating and drinking.

For the most part Silverstein was successful, but there were the usual crises.

Emerging from the pre-recording sessions with Irving Aaronson without incident, Mario was ready to embark on the actual shooting when he was commanded to attend a dinner in Naples. As outlandish as it seemed, the command came from the Mafia. This insidious organization harassed Mario through his whole stay in Italy. He never knew what it wanted of him, or what he should do.

He went to the dinner, and while he was there something set him off on a binge. When he returned home, late at night, Betty rebuked him. Mario's condition became so serious that he was hospitalized. Silverstein, on a short trip to New York, immediately flew back to Rome to see what could be done.

When he saw Silverstein, Mario broke into a fit of crying. Though he was under heavy sedation, he seemed to sense that once again he was betraying his obligations.

"Red, I swear to you I'll finish this picture," Mario said, sobbing.

Silverstein believed Mario, as I had so often in the past. But this time Mario kept his promise.

For the rest of Mario's stay in the hospital, two ex-GI medical students kept watch over him outside his door. They had no trouble with Mario, but when he returned to work he still had trouble taking the simplest of orders.

Silverstein was ready and willing to use every device to insure the completion of *Seven Hills* and to restore Mario's reputation as an international singing favorite. When he sensed that he was going to need help to keep Mario from going overboard again, he asked Dr. Bill Cahan, of the *Winged Victory* troupe, to write Mario a straight-talk letter about his behavior. The doctor gladly obliged. Soon after, when he visited Rome, he looked up Mario.

Mario was happy to see his friend of Army days, and they spent a few hours talking about old times. Suddenly Mario said, "That was quite a letter you sent me."

"I hope you understood it, for your own good," said Dr. Cahan.

Mario dropped the subject as quickly as he had brought it up. "Well, Bill, have you liked my movies?"

"I've never seen one," said Bill with a laugh.

"Why not?" said Mario, pretending to be hurt.

"Have you ever seen any of my cancer operations?"

The two men roared. When the doctor left, Silverstein was convinced Mario would behave for the duration of the filming. He did.

When the cameras stopped grinding on *Seven Hills*, Mario expressed his gratitude to Red with a magnificent watch. Engraved on the back of it were the words: THANKS FOR A NEW LIFE.

Soon it seemed that the new life was off to a good start, for reviews of *Seven Hills* praised Mario's "compelling voice" and insisted his return meant "box office." *Variety* called the movie a vocal "tour-de-force," praised Mario's impressions of Perry Como, Dean Martin, and Frankie Laine, and even noticed that he had gotten his weight down to meet the standards.

"He appears far more relaxed than ever before," said A. H. Weiler of *The New York Times*, "and he sings up a storm." Weiler, too, was delighted with Mario's imitations.

Returning from what could be considered a triumphal tour of Rome, Silverstein, at Mario's request, got in touch with me. He wanted to find out if I would be interested in going to Rome to conduct for Mario's recordings.

"Mario has ambitious plans," Red told me. "He wants to make more pictures, and I think he really means business now. He talks about a concert tour, too."

I was thrilled. It almost seemed that Rome *had* worked a miracle on Mario. At the time I was conducting for the New York City Center Opera Company, but I felt I had to go to Rome to be with Mario again.

I asked Julius Rudel, General Director of the City Center, if he would release me from; my contract for the remainder of the season. He generously consented to do so.

Then I phoned Mario in Rome.

"Costa, you must come here," he said. "I'm singing like ten tigers." I told him I would, and he promised to send me money for transportation.

After waiting a week for the money, I became alarmed. Having already severed my working relationship with the City Center, I was without a job. Was this the same old Mario, after all?

I ran into Julius Rudel one day in the street. "I thought you were in Rome with Mario Lanza," he said.

When I explained what had happened, he was kind enough to let me start the season with the City Center.

About a month later, in October, I got a call from Betty. She told me General Artists Management had my money for the overseas trip, that I should contact them at once and leave for Rome.

When I arrived, Mario was brisk, trim, fresh-faced and ebullient. He looked better than I had seen him look for years. I was amazed and delighted.

And I was pleased and reassured by the happy relationship between Mario and Betty. I had seen the bitterness and hostility between them and had suspected that was the normal state of their marriage. I had heard the stories about Betty drugging Mario's drinks and refused to believe them. Seeing them together now like a man and wife on a second honeymoon, listening to their animated talk of Italy and the future, I had to brush aside all such theories and believe simply what I was seeing.

We went into the Excelsior Hotel, where I was to be Mario's guest till I found quarters. In the cocktail lounge Betty and I ordered drinks; Mario didn't take a thing. Involuntarily I nodded in approval.

Mario noticed my nod. "I don't want to look at the stuff," he assured me. "I'm off it forever!"

Then we went to the Madison Restaurant for supper. Mario ate only a steak and a salad without oil.

"This has been my diet for a long time," he said. "I intend to keep it that way. No more abusing myself with all those rich foods. Just good simple foods for me."

If Mario's assurances had a hollow ring, I could not dispute, and I did not want to dispute, the evidence I saw before me. Mario was fit and happy.

When I was told we were going to London for the Command Performance at the Palladium, I became the optimist again, in defiance of all I knew and all my disappointments.

Then came Mario's terrible three-day orgy in London. It was incredible that he managed to go through with his performance. But it was a final turning point in my mind. No longer would I let myself be persuaded by sentiment on emotion. I recognized the enormity of Mario's problem. It would not pass away. Mario was going to destroy himself, and it was only a matter of time till he succeeded.

21. Mixed Receptions

*O*N NEW YEAR'S EVE Mario, his spirits temporarily revived, felt he had good reason to celebrate.

Only a few weeks before, Leslie Grade had induced him to appear in a television show from London's Palladium. Controlling his urges to drink and run away, Mario carried it off excellently. The show marked the first live TV singing role of Mario's career.

Then Bill Judd of Columbia Artists came to London and sounded out Mario on his feelings about a European concert tour. When Mario expressed his eagerness for the idea, it didn't take long for Judd to discover that Mario had not been forgotten. By

December 20, 1957, the tour was booked solid through March, 1958.

Having watched Mario's three days of hell in London, and unable to erase that impression from his mind, Peter Pritchard flew to Rome to get reassurance.

"Do you think Mario is up to it?" Peter asked me warily but hopefully.

"I'm not clairvoyant," I said, "but right now he seems fine." What more could I say?

So the hour was set, and Christmas and New Year's Eve became a time for hope and merriment in Mario's household. There was a huge Christmas tree, so tall that it almost touched the ceiling of the armory-like living room. It was garnished with toys and bulbs and decorations. The food, from the rizo in brodo and the calamaretti through the roast chicken, the lasagna, steak, gnioche, and the mozarella cheese to the tortoni to the demitasse, was the best, as Mario always insisted it must be.

On New Year's Eve the precious black caviar was marched in at midnight in three-pound tin boxes. The crisp toast, chopped onion and lemon were there, too, so that it could be eaten properly. The children were permitted to stay up for the festivities. At Mario's suggestion the youngsters formed a quartet and I directed them. They made Mario roar with fatherly delight.

But the most fun was yet to come. In Rome on New Year's Eve it has long been the custom to add to the uncontrolled bedlam by throwing noisy objects out of the windows, between the hours of eleven and one in the morning. Mario was only too willing to do as the Romans do; he had saved odds and ends for weeks for the occasion, and now the children joined him as he pelted the streets outside the villa with an assortment of glass and junk.

A few days later the European concert tour was ready to start. "It's going to be a bigger success than *The Great Caruso* tour," said Mario.

In my heart I knew it would not be so, that nothing would ever be the same again for Mario. He would never recapture the past, no matter how hard he tried. His only hope for the future was the opera. Perhaps it was his only hope for true happiness, too. But it was unattainable. I knew that and would not say it.

But how could I think anything else when, in the first moments after settling in our compartment on the train for England, Mario called in the porter and ordered beer. I made up my mind I wouldn't argue or try to persuade. I knew it was useless, that I was dealing with a sick man, a man incapable of saving himself from tragedy.

At our first concert in Sheffield, England, Mario looked well and was in good voice. The tickets were sold out in a few hours, and many were turned away. His fans haunted the hotel till three in the morning merely to get a glimpse of him.

Mario peeked out of his hotel window. "See, Costa," he said, "I told you, it's the *Caruso* tour all over again."

Some of Mario's relatives lived in Glasgow, so a concert was booked there, at St. Andrew's Hall. Mario was beside himself with joy to discover waiters with Italian-Scotch accents and he tipped them in pounds. Baffled by pounds, half crowns, shillings and pence, Mario continued to strew them with abandon around the countryside. When I tried to explain their values or curtail his spending, Mario would say, "I don't know the difference, and I don't care."

Though we had no concert scheduled for Edinburgh, when we passed through we were invited to have caviar and strawberry tarts at the Caledonia Hotel. Mario insisted on accepting, for he had heard that the hotel also served the finest Nova Scotia salmon.

After lunch, as we were preparing to leave, Mario noticed a line of people standing outside the revolving door of the hotel. "Where did they come from? Who told them I was in town?" Mario asked. He was so pleased he wanted to burst out in song right there in the lobby.

I was pleased, too, until I realized that the crowd hadn't come to see Mario at all. As we walked through the revolving door, I turned to look back into the hotel lobby. A newlywed couple was traipsing down the stairs and the people who had queued up to "see Mario" rushed forward to greet their friends. To the day he died Mario believed that the people in Edinburgh had heard he was passing through the city and had come out to see him, as they would any visiting dignitary.

We did five other concerts elsewhere in England, then returned to London for a few days of rest. There were three concerts set for the huge Albert Hall, and we wanted to have Mario in the best frame of mind for them.

Covered by a glass dome 155 feet high, Albert Hall is 273 feet long and by far the largest assembly hall in Great Britain. Seating 8,000 people, with room for many standees, the hall has been used for everything from Philharmonic concerts to prize fights to World War II reunions. Some Britishers look upon it as a "mausoleum." In a way, whatever was left of our hopes for Mario were buried here, too. But that didn't happen until the third concert in February.

The night of the first concert at Albert Hall, Mario's old agitation was plain to see on the surface. But he demonstrated enough will power and discipline to refrain from drinking. Before going on he phoned Betty and the kids. "The English are just great. They love me, and I love them. We sold out the Albert Hall in a hurry."

As Mario walked out on the stage and into a great ovation, I could see the vastness of the arena hit him with a terrible impact. He whispered to me: "Have you ever seen such a joint? It gives me the creeps."

"It's no different from any place else," I said. "Don't think about it."

"It's too big, Costa."

"Listen to the applause," I said. "They're crazy about you. You'll do fine."

I took a deep breath and crossed my fingers. Please, God, I thought, let him get through this without breaking; let him be good, let them like him.

He was good, and they did like him. They pleaded for encores of "Because You're Mine" and "La donna è mobile." When he hit his high B, the cheers were deafening.

As he stood there acknowledging the applause, I said softly in his ear, "I told you, Mario. It's no different here from any other place. There are just more people to appreciate you."

His face strained and perspiring, Mario smiled over at me. What relief he must have felt at surviving this first performance in the Albert Hall!

We had our next date for Munich, Germany, on January 27, 1958. We planned to go by air from London, though Mario still hated and feared flying. He drank heavily before getting on the plane and continued while the plane was in flight. When we arrived, he was almost immovable. I had to prod him and help him as we left the plane.

At the end of the Munich concert, the enthusiastic Germans converged on the stage, making it almost impossible for us to get off. At one time this kind of response from his fans would have been a sheer delight to Mario. Now it was unnerving, upsetting.

Afraid the audience might react the same way at Stuttgart, Mario asked me to make an announcement before the concert that he would gladly sing encores if they promised not to rush the stage at the end. I made the announcement. But the spectators broke their promise, and moved on Mario.

By the time we escaped, Mario was exhausted. It wasn't like him. Something was wrong.

Mario knew that he was ill, and the doctors confirmed it. They told him his blood pressure was high and that he was suffering from phlebitis in his left leg. They urged him to cut short the tour and return to Rome. Our concerts at Hamburg and Baden-Baden were postponed; we flew back to Italy.

The painful inflammation in his leg was causing Mario great distress, so he consented to a short period of hospitalization in Rome. He had to take injections daily, and a rubber stocking was placed on the leg. When he got out of bed he had to walk with a cane.

While he was in the hospital a British newspaper printed a story that Mario actually had nothing wrong with him, that he was being seen all over Rome in night clubs, and that he had no reason to be running out on concert dates.

This was one of those striking ironies in Mario's life. When, in the past, he had had no excuse for canceling or breaking engagements, nobody had questioned his health or his whereabouts. Now that he had a valid excuse for postponing his commitments, reporters were making up preposterous lies about him.

A revamped tour was prepared for Mario by March, 1958, when his health seemed to be better. Mario decided that whenever possible we would travel by train rather than car, so that he could relax completely. He also decided that he would remain quiet the day of and the day before a concert.

"The only time I'll make a sound is at our concerts," said Mario. "Then I'll make sounds that nobody will forget."

Mario followed this novel program as best he could, writing what he wanted to say on a pad. Our poker games were fantastic exercises in silence. When Mario lost—and these days his luck seemed to be bad, even at the card table—he would scrawl an uncomplimentary remark about me on his pad. For reporters in England who asked proper questions he wrote decent answers; for anyone who asked about his weight he would pencil an angry epithet and shove it under his nose.

Mario's silent routine had its amusing moments. One day a young English girl in her teens, one of two chiefs of the "Magic Mario Club" who were following us about on our British tour, cornered Mario while he was trying to rest in his hotel room.

"You don't have much hair on your chest," she said.

No, I don't, Mario scribbled on his pad. *But Costa does.*

219

There were other moments that helped us forget the daily struggle and strain of touring. For one, in a cold concert hall in Manchester, Mario became so annoyed with an unruly crowd that he sat down on the stage next to me and said, "Let's play cards, until they shut up." And then there was the Scotch tailor episode.

When Mario outgrew his tuxedo, we visited a tailor in Edinburgh to have a new pair of trousers made up for him. As the Scot took Mario's measurements, we caught a whiff of good Scotch "dew" on his breath and expected difficulty. When the trousers arrived, we knew we had been right.

We sent the trousers back to the tailor, encouraging him to sober up before trying again.

But the next fitting wasn't much better: as gross as Mario had become, the trousers were still too big and baggy.

Instead of flying into a rage at the man's incompetence, Mario laughed and said, "Here, have a glass of beer with us."

"All I drink is Scotch," retorted the tailor.

So Scotch was brought in for him, and the Scotsman proposed a toast: "May you never need a doctor."

This stubborn, independent little man had appealed to Mario from the start; and that toast made Mario his friend. Mario loved the trousers, and in days to come he wore them as a gesture of defiance on the concert stage.

Meanwhile, on the sober side, a series of acrimonious debates over fees had been going on between Mario's agents and myself. I couldn't point to any written contract with Mario: a handshake had always been enough for us. Mario had always been generous and thoughtful. But now his representatives didn't want to pay my usual fees. I objected strenuously, and only out of loyalty to Mario was I willing to keep working until a solution was reached. Mario himself did not enter the negotiations.

I was sorry that I had become involved in such a situation, for I knew it would touch my working relationship with Mario. It had to, and it did.

We were due to play the Albert Hall again on February 16, 1958, and since we had had such a tumultuous reception in Belfast, where we performed before 10,000, I looked forward to another great night.

But the tension and fear that had gripped Mario before the first two Albert Hall dates returned again—compounded, I felt sure, by the conflict over my fees. Hours before the concert started, I knew we were in for a bad evening.

Mario had been drinking all day. Backstage, when I met him in his dressing room, he was sullen, his face flushed from hours of ale. Testing his voice, he was embarrassed to hear ungodly sounds come out.

On stage Mario rocked uncertainly. I was close enough to see his bloodshot eyes and quivering lips. My heart pounded for Mario. How bad would he be?

Before he began his first number, he turned to me, glared hatefully, then sneered, "The boy wants my money."

I ignored him, pretending not to have heard what he said.

When he began to sing, it was simply a question of how tolerant the audience would be. All that was left that night was the scar tissue of a once phenomenal voice. He never should have gone on;

it would have been far better for him to have canceled out, to have gone back to the hotel to drink himself into a coma.

Mario himself realized how bad it was. After two selections, he walked uncertainly to the front of the stage.

"I am very sorry tonight," he told the crowd, "but while house hunting in your beloved London the other day, I slipped and injured my ribs. Will you please forgive me?"

It was not a pretty scene.

Mario finished his performance, but at the end the audience hadn't forgiven him. Mario's excuses had caught up with him.

Despite the reverse at Albert Hall, the tour continued. Mario tried often to tell me he was sorry for what he had said to me that night. There was never any doubt in my mind that I would go on with him. I knew he needed me more than ever.

In Paris, our concert was at the Olympia Theatre, where Edith Piaf has staged many shows. Mario was again below par, singing only six numbers, which made the Parisians somewhat fretful.

After three days in Paris, Mario was presented with a hotel bill of over $1,000. The long-distance calls Mario was making to Rome and California, the food he was serving to innumerable acquaintances and hangers-on, the service he had demanded and received night and day, must have added up to that figure. But Mario was angry and protested the sum. To keep the peace the management lopped $100 oil the bill, and Mario paid. But he kept on cursing the hotel for cheating him.

Mario's voice was better in Ostend. In Rotterdam our concert was in a hall with poor acoustics and a dismal heating system. It was brutal to sing in such a place, yet Mario fared better here than he had in Albert Hall. His fee was only $1,000 as opposed to the $2,000 and $5,000 he'd been earning on this tour.

In a state of discouragement, with Mario drinking heavily and complaining of a sore throat, we set out for Germany. But in Hanover, Mario suddenly appeared in good voice again. He seemed, that night, and a few nights later in the mammoth indoor stadium in Kiel, Germany, to be at the peak of his powers as a singer. His voice, "darker" and richer than I had heard it in years, thrilled me. Its volume and substance rivaled any male voice I had ever heard in my life.

I couldn't believe what I was hearing. This was the man I had thought was through.

"It was torture for me last night," Mario told me the morning after the Kiel concert. "That damn sore throat of mine, I can't get rid of it."

"I don't know how you did it," I said, "but I think you were better than during the *Caruso* tour."

"Do you mean it, Costa?" he said eagerly.

"Yes."

"Well, you wait. I'll show 'em—I'll show 'em all."

22. Fiasco at Hamburg

$\mathcal{F}$OR months, as Mario's problems became more obvious to all, and harder to control, I was being worn down to raw nerves. I had played nursemaid, straight man, watchdog, handyman, and chaperon so long that my own usefulness was being seriously impaired. I felt that in another month, or a week, I could crack wide open.

I made up my mind now to limit my relationships with Mario to those hours when I played for him or rehearsed with him. I wanted discreetly to absent myself during the drinking bouts, the brawls with women, the wild and destructive rages.

I wasn't running away from anything. I was merely admitting how little I could do for Mario now, and trying to preserve my ability to do it.

Alex Revides, a Shakespearean actor with whom Mario had been friendly in Rome, now became the helping hand in Mario's hectic life. Alex tried his best, but he failed to realize that Mario could not be pressed when he was drinking.

We were scheduled to do a concert in Hamburg, Germany, on the night of April 16, 1958. In Mario's hotel room at the Vier Jahriszeiten a discussion started between Alex and Mario about Otello, the role that Mario wanted most to sing on the operatic stage. The volume of beer and conversation increased to guzzling and shouting. When I thought my head would burst, I got up to leave.

"Remember, Mario," I said from the door, "we sing tomorrow. Go to bed soon." I left the problem to Alex.

At five o'clock the next morning they were still going strong, with Mario yelling and singing at the top of his lungs. During the night Mario must have sung the most dramatic arias of *Otello* a dozen times; and there had been dozens of complaints from residents of the hotel. Finally, Mario fell into a drunken stupor, and it wasn't till noon that he awakened.

When I stopped by his room, I knew what I'd find. But I hadn't expected that Mario would already have called a specialist to examine his raw throat. Another doctor was called in for consultation. Between them they thought they might be able to clear up the inflammation. Shaking my head, I left for a session of practice at the concert hall.

When I returned to the hotel the doctors were still ministering to Mario. I told myself it was just one more concert that Mario wouldn't make. I wasn't bitter, just cynical and resigned. Meanwhile, Collins, the manager of the Hamburg hall, was still unaware of Mario's condition: it had been kept a secret—if anything can be a secret after two doctors and an accompanist know about it.

I went through the motions, the formalities. I dressed for the concert. Then I went to Mario's suite.

The doctors told us, "If you want to endanger his voice permanently, then let him sing. If you want to protect his voice, make him stay here."

The concert, set for 8:15, was canceled at 7:55. When the manager learned of the decision he rushed to the hotel in despair. Surrounded by the doctors, the manager, the mayor of Hamburg, and Revides, Mario lay abed looking like a little boy who has been caught stealing cookies, and I stood there trying to think of something to say to the people waiting at the Musik Halle.

"I'll go and tell them that Mario is sick," I said to the manager.

"It won't do," Collins warned. "They're in a dangerous mood. This is Mario's second postponement in Hamburg."

"I'll take my chances," I said.

With a last look at Mario, I left for the hall.

When I got there, I saw that Collins was right. The crowd was jeering, threatening, throwing programs in the air.

As I wandered onto the stage the taunts increased. Collins walked front and center, signaling for quiet.

"I want to introduce," he said in German, "Mr. Constantine Callinicos—"

The moment he got my name out of his mouth, the crowd went wild with its derisive shrieking and howling. During the *Caruso* tour I thought I had seen everything in the way of unruly, obnoxious behavior, but I had to go to Hamburg to see my first concert-hall "lynch mob."

They came at me, pressing up to the stage, milling around me, shoving and stamping. Photographers had climbed on top of the grand piano and were snapping away at me. An elbow caught me in the ribs.

Now they were yelling "damned Amerikaner" at me, and a hundred other oaths in German.

I heard somebody cry, "Play the piano, maybe they'll stop!" But I couldn't get within ten feet of it. Then someone shouted in Greek, "Tell Lanza he's no damn good!"

For a long time I stood there transfixed by the ferment and uproar. Then, my heart palpitating, my hands trembling, I worked my way backstage. With a police escort, I was at last on my way out of the hall.

When I reached the hotel, the police had posted sentries at the entrance and in the rear. Rumors had spread through the city that the hotel was going to be stormed and Mario seized. What a nightmare—I couldn't believe any of it was happening.

As I let myself in upstairs, there were the doctors and Revides; Mario was on the phone telling Betty how well he felt, how fine

228

everything was. When he saw me, he blew a kiss to Betty and said good-by.

"I heard all about it, Costa," Mario roared, slamming down the receiver. "They almost killed you, didn't they? It took guts, Costa. Thanks for helping me out."

I told Mario in Greek what I thought of him.

Mario clapped his thigh with glee. "If you could only see yourself, you'd laugh till your sides hurt!"

"My sides hurt enough as it is," I said sullenly.

We made reservations to leave Hamburg by plane at seven the next morning. There were wails and protests from Mario's managers, who wanted him to stay and continue the tour, but his only concern was to get out of town alive. Later Mario was sued for four cancellations, including the one at Hamburg.

23. When the Next Drink Might Kill

*W*ITH the Germans and his British manager suing Mario for his cancellations, with hotel managers in several countries threatening suit over Mario's unpaid bills, and with Mario himself swearing to sue a British newspaperman, Mario was hard pressed for money. So he determined to go through with another motion picture. Producer Alexander Gruter of Corona Films in Munich closed a deal with Mario to make a movie called *For the First Time*, which would turn out to be Mario's last film in his life. Mario was to receive $200,000, plus a percentage of the profits, and in consideration of his immediate needs for cash, he was to be advanced $8,000 a month.

Before production of the movie began, Mario was deluged with concert offers from South Africa, New Zealand, Australia-everywhere. The guarantees ran as high as $10,000 per concert. Coming in the face of adverse publicity, these offers surprised me. But not Mario. With a shrug he'd say, "The more notorious you are, the more they want you."

The offer from South Africa was especially attractive, and the promoters went so far as to deposit money for Mario in Rome banks. So despite the prospect of air travel, Mario could not resist. It wasn't two weeks after the Hamburg fiasco that Mario and I began to prepare for our South African invasion.

Every morning at ten we started practice, and it went fairly well. But on the slightest provocation, and sometimes without any, Mario would explode. One day, while we were rehearsing in the music room, Mario heard little Marco playing Daddy's Christmas records in another room. "I can't stand listening to myself sing those damn Christmas records any more," Mario cried out. "Tell him to stop before I blow my top." And each explosion unnerved Mario for hours.

Gruter suggested to Mario that he should go to Walchensee in the Bavarian Alps before starting work on the picture. "You'll love it there," said the producer. "It's magnificent country, full of Bavarian villages, mountains, forests and a huge lake. You'll be able to rest there and get in shape for the movie." Gruter was neither naive nor misinformed; he was trying to ward off trouble.

But Mario was insistent: he wanted to do the concert tour in South Africa first, then proceed with the movie. But once again Mario was monstrously overweight, and one hour before we were supposed to get on the Britannia jet for the 20-hour trip, he pulled out of the deal.

I was crushed. I had been relying on the fees from the South African tour to regain solvency. Now I was left without a penny.

By July, 1958, Mario's health was in a precarious state. His phlebitis was bothering him; he ignored his diet; and he had become enamored of a new drink—Campari, an Italian *apéritif*—which he consumed in enormous quantities.

Many days Mario never emerged from the kitchen. Here he could eat and drink to his heart's content. Here he didn't have to speak to anyone, or risk censure or criticism. I would shudder when I saw him trudge oil to the kitchen. I knew that meant practice for the day was at an end and the Campari drunk was beginning.

Trying fitfully to lose weight, Mario submitted to mercurial diuretic injections, which can make the body yield large amounts of water and salt. He also started, on doctor's advice, to take little white antabuse tablets. Antabuse, as I learned, was a drug that had been first released for general use around 1951 to fight alcoholism. After taking an antabuse tablet, the average person would react violently to any alcoholic beverage; he'd be apt to suffer from severe shortness of breath; his face would flush purple in a matter of minutes; a disconcertingly rapid pulse would ensue. For others, perhaps heavier drinkers, the reaction was even more alarming. Nausea would bring on certain manifestations of cardiac stress (dyspnea), and a coma could occur.

Subjecting himself to such torture did not faze Mario. On the one hand he continued to take the antabuse, and on the other, he continued to drink. It was painful to be a spectator at this crazy battle between the poison and the antidote. Mario's face would turn beet red, then sheet white. Then, while he struggled to breathe, he would cry out in anguish for Betty. She couldn't bear to watch what he was going through, and, sadly, she would often refuse to come to him. The more he needed her, the less she had to do with him.

Sometimes the symptoms lasted for hours, sometimes for days. Since the intensity of reaction depends on both the dosage of the drug and the amount of alcohol ingested, we often found ourselves waiting morbidly to see how much Mario drank and how many tablets he decided to take.

Finally, unable to cope with Mario, we called Dr. Morica of the Valle Giulia Clinic and begged him to find a solution to the problem.

Dr. Morica tried his best. "I warn you, Mario," he said. "Keep this up just a little longer and you will be dead."

"Hell, I've got a strong constitution," Mario replied. "I'll beat this thing. No goddam pills are going to kill Mario Lanza." Then he struck the pose of a prize fight winner and flexed his flabby muscles. I had to turn away at the infantile sight.

Any professional, financial or household crisis now became an excuse for him to embark on maddening rounds of orgies. He developed such a tolerance for antabuse that the drug had little effect on him.

Each time he emerged from a beer or Campari binge, whether it lasted an hour, a day, a week, or three weeks, Mario would swear off drink. But now that he was a true alcoholic, forcing the servants to smuggle bottles to him and to dispose of empties, nothing could be done with him. Not even music moved him. When I played the piano for him, he'd sit sunken into a big armchair, with his legs resting on an ottoman. Invariably, he would fall asleep after a while and begin mumbling, "Everything will be all right . . . just wait and see . . . we'll do it . . ."

Gruter, in a state of alarm over the fate of his movie, tried in vain to get through to Mario. Finally, Gruter and I agreed that Mario's last best chance was Walchensee, where alcoholics as well as overweight people had been helped by sustained treatment. Walchensee's two-week sleep diet, during which time a person is fed intravenously, had become famous throughout Europe. We had to get Mario to Walchensee. I resolved to catch Mario early in the morning, before he shut out the world and began drinking. Perhaps, then, he'd listen.

One morning at 9:30 I did find him in fairly good spirits. "Mario, my friend," I began, "you know that you're killing yourself, don't you?"

"Forget it, Costa," he answered.

"I can't forget it. We watch this go on, day in, day out, and we wonder how long you can last."

"I have an indestructible body," he said, "You know that."

"I don't know any such thing. No man is indestructible, you know that."

"I know that, Costa," he said, suddenly repentant. "But I'm so terribly unhappy. When I'm happy I don't do these things."

I asked him what made him unhappy. The list that he ticked off included broken promises made to him by friends, his troubles with Betty, his troubles with Sam Weiler, his last movie, his next movie, the producers he had worked for, the people who had plotted against him.

"Listen to me," I said in despair. "For your own good, I have something I want to suggest to—"

"Please, Costa," he interrupted wearily. "Tell me tomorrow. I won't be so low tomorrow. Then we'll really begin to do a job. I'll be all right. Just don't think I'm crazy. It's just that I have to get away from all these troubles in my head."

Then his eyes glazed over, and the interview was at an end.

The next day Paul Baron, the conductor, came to the house and immediately he and Mario got into an argument over a recording. I happened to be in the room at the time. That was my misfortune, for Mario in his rage picked up the phone and hurled it in the air. Accidentally it hit my kneecap, causing me intense pain: for months after, my leg and then my back hurt. The only good that came of the accident was that the argument stopped. Mario couldn't find Words to express his apologies. I knew he hadn't meant to hurt me, but the damage was done.

Somehow Gruter finally got his way with Mario. Mario agreed to go to Walchensee and get in shape to film *For the First Time*. And, incredible as it seemed, he actually went to Walchensee.

With Mario in capable hands, I took a trip to see the director of the Stuttgart Opera. When I returned to Munich, Al Panone, one of Mario's friends, called to advise me to go at once to Walchensee.

I left at once by car, arrived two hours later, and demanded to see the doctor in charge of Mario's case.

The German doctor studied me for a long moment, then asked how close I considered myself to Mario.

"I feel I am one of the best friends he has."

"Well," he began, taking a portentous drag on his pipe, "your friend is a very sick man. It's his liver. The next drink he takes might be his last. As a close friend, you would do well to explain this to him at once."

For a long time I had assumed as much, but now that I knew my assumption was correct, now that I was being charged with the responsibility of telling Mario the awful facts, I was numb with fear.

I took a room close to Mario, in the same cottage. Then I went in to see him.

"Costa!" Mario cried. "What the hell are you doing here? I thought you were in Stuttgart!" He was happy to see me, lonely and eager to have someone to talk to.

"I came to see the view," I said lamely, pointing to the postcard scene outside the window.

"It's all mine," said Mario. "It's paradise. I hate it."

"I think it's the most beautiful place I've seen."

"Join me in the supper special," he said, with a grimace. "We're having canned peaches and cottage cheese. Isn't that something to write home about?" He held his nose with the fingers of his right hand.

"Sounds good to me," I said. "I can stand losing la little weight, too."

"Come on, Costa," Mario said. "We'll have a beer. Hey, nurse!"

When the nurse arrived, Mario shouted, "Get us some beer!"

I'm sorry," she said, "but I have strict orders."

"Just one," he pleaded.

"It is impossible," she said, turning to leave.

Mario threw a curse after her. "She's one of those damn one-track Germans," he said.

On the way back from our Spartan supper, Mario suggested taking a walk. Before I could say no, we ran into Mario's doctor.

"Mr. Lanza," he said, a note of command in his voice, "you should be resting."

"I just wanted to go for a little walk. This country is good for my spirits."

"Mr. Lanza, you are to rest now." With that the doctor walked on.

Then Mario turned to me. "Costa, how about seeing what goes on in the village?"

The village was only a few hundred yards down the road. If the walk did not harm him, what lay at the end of the walk certainly would. There were taverns and restaurants in the little resort town. This is where Mario wanted to go, and I knew it.

Mario set out for town; I went along, struggling to organize in my mind what I must tell him. And he had to believe me.

When we got to town, Mario pointed to a typical German *Gaststätte*. "Let's go in here," he said.

"I just ate," I said. "So did you. And you must not drink."

"All I want is just one lousy beer," said Mario. "That dame back there was a fool. I can have a beer if I want to. They're all idiots up here. The mountain air gets them."

"Mario," I said desperately, "do you have any idea why I'm here?"

"Sure, you like the scenery," he kidded.

"No, I wish that was the reason. But it isn't. I came because you're—because you're in danger. It's your liver."

For a moment Mario paused. Then he grabbed my arm, like a policeman dealing with a mischief-maker. "Look, don't pay any attention to them. Doctors are the same every place you go." He relaxed his grip on my arm. "Come on, let's have a beer in that restaurant."

"Mario, would you drink that beer if there was a chance it might kill you?"

"Sure I would," he answered. "Hell, what harm can one beer do?"

"I'm telling you, Mario, the next drink you take might kill you!"

He laughed at me. "Just one, just one, then we'll go back and you can tuck me in bed."

"I don't want to be a party to your suicide."

"Just one for good health," he implored.

I couldn't talk him out of it. He was standing next to the restaurant now. Then he opened the ancient wooden door and walked in.

"Before you have your beer," I said as we sat down at a table covered with a checkerboard cloth, "would you listen to a story I want to tell you?"

"Sure, but make it short, I'm getting damned thirsty."

For years now I had wanted to tell Mario about a young man named Lansing Hatfield, with whom I had gone on a concert tour.

239

Lansing's problem had been drink; I tried but failed to curb his thirst. I didn't like to think of Lansing, but now I had to tell Mario his story. Perhaps it would touch him, make him stop. . . .

"Hatfield was a tall, handsome, talented baritone," I began. "Many said he showed great promise. He came from Hickory, North Carolina, and I toured with him in 1946, around the time I first met you. Lansing was already an alcoholic; he always carried a fifth in his pocket.

"We were in Bartlesville, Oklahoma, for a concert. A half hour before it was time to go to the concert hall, I went to his room, knocked on his door. There was no answer. Then, through the open transom, I could hear his snoring. He was mumbling something about finding matches on the train. Finally, I forced the door open.

"Lansing was lying on the bed in his street clothes. He was disheveled and unshaven. I closed the door, went downstairs, and out to the concert hall. I played a piano recital that night all by myself. I told the people that Lansing had laryngitis.

"A few weeks later I tried it with Lansing again, at Toronto, Canada. But he couldn't make it. He even drank in the shower room, where I couldn't keep tabs on him.

"Lansing died in August, 1954, Mario. He had cirrhosis of the liver and he was only thirty-eight years old."

When I finished, I discovered that my hands were trembling.

"Is that the end?" Mario said.

"Yes," I said. "Do you understand what I'm getting at, Mario?"

Mario's eyes narrowed, and the lines around his jaw hardened. "That's the last I ever want to hear about this guy Hatfield," he snarled. "He's got nothing to do with me."

Good God, I thought, hadn't I made my point? Doesn't he really care at all what happens to him?

"I just want you to know, Mario, that this can't keep on with you. You're killing yourself. I appeal to you now as one of my dearest and closest friends to stop this madness before it's too late. Don't go out the way Lansing did. Save yourself. Do it for your family. Do it for everyone who has ever heard your voice and admired your talent."

I was talked out. Perspiration rolled slowly down my forehead. And there Mario sat, a slow grin splitting his face from ear to ear. "I'll have that beer now," he said.

"I'm leaving," I said.

I got up to go. I felt dizzy, suddenly, and a dull headache was throbbing behind my eyes.

I walked toward the exit, turned once to see Mario gulping down the contents of a stein in one violent spasm.

He caught up with me on the road back to the sanatorium.

We walked along together for a few minutes without speaking. Finally, he said, "Next year we'll go to South America on the biggest tour of all. What a time we'll have!"

24. Near Midnight

$\mathcal{T}$HAT night, after Mario and I returned to our cottages, a heavy mist cloaked the countryside around Walchensee. Coaxed under the blankets by the welcome chill in the air, I should have slept soundly. But I was restive and troubled. My eyes scarcely closed for thinking that my mission had failed utterly, that in my presence Mario had taken a drink that might prove his last, that I had not stopped him.

As the first light of dawn filtered through my window, I slipped out of bed and dressed. Then I walked unsteadily to the door of my cottage. I had just opened the door when an apple-cheeked German youngster marched into view. I watched him trudge slowly along the gravel path leading past my cottage. Under his arm nestled a large bundle. I knew immediately what the young man was up to.

The boy knocked lightly on Mario's door, then entered. A few seconds later he emerged. The package was no longer under his arm.

Heartsick and panicky, I thought of storming into Mario's cottage and confiscating the bottle, and I thought of collaring the boy and giving him a tongue-lashing. But what was the use? As long as Mario wanted beer and could pay exorbitant tips, there would be other boys to bring him other bottles. With last night's drink he might already have succeeded in committing suicide.

Later on I did speak to the boy, and I told him in my best German that I had seen him enter Mario's cottage in the early hours of the morning.

He protested his innocence.

"Don't lie to me. If you do it again I'll report you to your superiors. It will cost you your job."

This threat seemed to frighten him. "I will not bring him more beer," he said with great reluctance.

Like a fool, the boy went directly to Mario's cottage to inform him that he couldn't bring beer any longer. From my room I could hear Mario lashing him with insults and curses. The boy didn't understand English but he knew that he was being bawled out by a master. When Mario saw that the boy would be of no further use, he shoved him out of the door.

Mario was still fuming when I knocked and walked in. "What the hell do you want?" he shouted.

I didn't answer.

"I only wanted a little beer," he complained. "What's wrong with that?"

I didn't answer. For a long time we faced each other without speaking.

"How about a game of cards?" Mario said finally.

"Deal," I said.

The next day Mario told me he was going to phone Betty and ask her to come to Walchensee with the kids. He did. Then he insisted that I order a piano from Munich, so we could start practicing again.

By the time the piano arrived I had moved to Munich, for Walchensee was too expensive. This meant I'd have to drive down each morning.

The day our work was to begin I arrived at ten. Mario, looking better than he had in weeks, couldn't wait to get on with it. We ran through operatic excerpts that he was scheduled to sing in *For the First Time*—the triumphal scene in *Aïda*, the deathbed scene in *Otello*, arias from Pagliacci, and the Trio from *Cosi fan Tutte*.

Embarking for the hundredth time on a rigid diet, this one approved by the doctor, Mario lived on *chatka* (imported crabmeat) soaked with paprika, steak, green salad, and skimmed milk.

When his family came, Mario was overjoyed. Each morning he played with the children, swam in the lake, rehearsed, then shopped in nearby Garmisch. Betty had brought the training equipment along, and Mario eagerly began lifting weights, doing push-ups and roadwork. Gruter, musical director Georgie Stoll, and director Rudy Mate made regular visits to discuss *For the First Time*. Mario seemed to be the happiest man in the world; and, fascinated by the beauty of the place, he often expressed a desire to stay there for the rest of his life.

But finally, after Mario had been at the resort for over seven weeks, we came back to Rome. It was late August of 1958.

I was assigned to the movie as operatic conductor. The next day we went to the Rome Opera House to make our recordings with the 160-member Rome Opera Orchestra, plus soloists and chorus from the Rome Opera.

After Mario recorded his first number, the *Aïda* triumphal scene, there was a burst of surprised excitement from the orchestra members, who till then had accepted the widespread notion that Mario's voice was strictly a product of Hollywood sound engineers.

"Why doesn't Mario come to sing with us here at the Opera House?" they asked.

Maestro Ricardo Vitale, the General Director of the Rome Opera, was generous in his praise of Mario and invited him back to open a season.

"I will sing here someday," said Mario. "Don't worry. I will be back."

As soon as my stint for the picture was completed, I prepared to leave Rome and return to my conducting job with the New York City Opera Company. I was asked to play the part of a conductor in the movie, but my work in New York was more important to me.

I said good-by to Mario and the family.

"You're yourself again, Mario," I said. "Good boy—keep it up."

For the First Time, which went before the cameras soon after, was shot in Italy, Germany, and Austria. Through it all Mario's behavior was relatively restrained, and he did not require the close supervision he'd had in *The Seven Hills of Rome*. Though the critical reception of the picture was not good, the consensus was that Mario's voice was amazingly rich and big. Even those who criticized Mario's operatic efforts did not belittle his natural talents.

In December, 1958, I returned to Rome expecting to work with Mario on more recordings. Arthur Brauner, another German producer, was ready to do a movie called *Granada*, and I thought I'd be asked to work with Mario on this project, too. There was no work for me. By this time Paul Baron had become something of a permanent member of Mario's camp, and a Neapolitan song album and a *Student Prince* album that Mario and I had planned to do together were now promised to Paul.

However, Mario was feeling unwell again, so I decided to remain in Rome for a while. In April, 1959, Mario checked into the hospital. He was desperately tired, and his eyes seemed to be receding deep into his head. His color was pasty, and the great swatches of fat that once yielded so quickly to his Spartan diets now clung to him stubbornly.

In April, before I left for Athens to conduct the Athens Symphony Orchestra, Mario asked me from his hospital bed to keep in touch, because he knew he'd need me. While I was in Athens, I continued to call him, but Mario kept reassuring me he was all right.

"I'll be out of the hospital next week," he told me one day. "I want you to come back to Rome then, because everybody's giving me trouble."

Reports reached me in Athens that Mario was walking out of recording sessions and drinking again.

Peter Lind Hayes, on a visit to Rome to tape some material, looked up his friend of *On the Beam* days. He was quite shocked with Mario's appearance.

"He told me he was dieting," said Peter. "But then I went to one of his extra special parties, where everybody and his brother were invited. Mario swigged down a whole bottle of champagne in less time than it took me to say hello. That was his way of dieting. Then he began to play his own records, singing along with them at the top of his lungs. I had the feeling he was beyond the pale, uncontrolled and uncontrollable."

I was back in Rome by June, 1959.

Now something new, and in a way humorous, had been added to Mario's life. An enterprising con man named Glenn Dale Castle, who later boasted he had issued over a million in bad checks and spent 28 years of his life merchandising everything but honesty under two dozen aliases and through two dozen arrests, had ingratiated himself to Mario.

Castle told Mario that he was Dudley Nichols, a famous Hollywood film writer. Mario had never known Nichols in Hollywood, but he knew that Dudley was a respected member of his trade and also an Oscar-winner.

Before Mario introduced me to Dudley he assured me how diffident his new friend was, in spite of all his attainments. "He never wants to talk about his credits. Mention his movies and he changes the subject. He's a marvelous person."

"Nichols" then told me that he was fed up with Hollywood and had come to Rome to retire—and perhaps to engage in a few side businesses. He expressed a strong interest in Mario's career. He said, "Mario has had terrible publicity too long, and most of it undeserved. I'd like to straighten out his relations with the press. I'm sure I can do it."

Also claiming to be a member of Alcoholics Anonymous, Castle promised Mario he would work with him on his drinking problem. Castle had a solution for all the world's ills, especially Mario's.

In a few weeks Mario opened an office with Castle just a block away from his villa. Castle suggested that an excellent business for Mario would be the manufacture of cigarette lighters. Mario, who might have had a head for business if he spent any time at it, promptly envisioned a new life for himself.

One day Castle, after hearing me play the piano, told me he was working on a biography of Chopin, and "I'll let you play the background music for the movie."

"I'd be delighted," I said.

"My wife used to be a pianist, too," he said.

A few days later I told Mario about the plan.

"Dudley's just crazy for your playing," said Mario.

I thought how nice it was for "Nichols" to have expressed such an interest in my ability. Never questioning his identity, I still felt there were certain inconsistencies about his background.

When "Nichols" showed me some of his writings, I secretly thought they were quite bad, entirely unprofessional. I told Mario my opinion.

"Oh, I guess old Dudley has had it as a writer," Mario said. "He ought to stick to our business now."

For the next few weeks Mario's association with this incomparably gifted fraud went sailing along at a merry pace. When the two of them weren't at their office, Nichols was feasting at Mario's house and spinning interminable stories about his prowess with women.

One evening, while a party was going on full force at Mario's villa, a girl who had known the real Dudley Nichols in Hollywood was introduced to his namesake. She said nothing to Castle but waited until she was alone with Mario.

"This man that you're so friendly with, Mario," she began. "Do you know much about him?"

"I know that he's a great talent and we're going to make a million together," beamed Mario.

"I hate to disappoint you, but I knew the *real* Dudley Nichols in California. I worked with him. This is not Dudley Nichols. This is a fake!"

Mario was determined to look into the matter. He contacted his Hollywood business manager, Myrt Blum, and asked him for a clarification of the "Dudley Nichols" situation.

Blum located the real Dudley Nichols in California and informed Mario that he must have a phony on his hands. Unfortunately, the real Nichols was recuperating from an ailment at the time and could not go to Rome himself to unmask his masquerader.

Now that he was on to Castle's game, Mario decided to play one himself. When pictures of the real Nichols arrived, Mario told a reporter for the Rome *Daily American* that Dudley Nichols would soon be coming to Rome, and that they could publish this information, along with a photo he would be glad to provide for them.

The story was printed a few days later, with the picture beside it. That marked the end of Mario's relationship with his latest mentor.

Later, when I visited Castle's "business" office, I discovered that Mario had been using it as a front, too: the refrigerator in the corner was well stocked with beer. Tired of having to sneak drinks in his own home, Mario simply went to the office and did his guzzling out of range of friends and family.

At this time George Marek, an RCA executive, came to Rome, had dinner with Mario, and suggested that Mario make some new records of *The Vagabond King*, *The Desert Song*, *The Merry Widow*, and re-record *The Great Caruso* for stereophonic sound. Mario agreed and said he also wanted to do an album of sacred songs.

In July, Mario and I started our recordings of *The Vagabond King* at the Cine Città studio.

In one night, from five till eleven, we made every recording—twelve songs in all. It was our best and most harmonious session, and Mario was magnificent. After each song was finished, Mario looked for applause from Betty and the children in the control booth. They gave it lavishly.

While Mario was in a magnanimous mood, I pressed to start work on our next project, *The Desert Song*. We began on the score in the last days of July. By the beginning of August, all appeared ready. I went ahead and scheduled the first recording session. My fingers were crossed, but my hopes were as high as they had been for months.

At the first recording session Mario was at his best. Unfortunately, however, the contractor had assembled a mediocre orchestra, so we were able to complete only two songs. But by the time another contractor had put together a good orchestra, Mario had reverted to his drinking habits again. So we failed miserably to complete our work in a second session.

As we assembled for our third recording session, I had premonitions that Mario's condition would deter us from finishing our work. I made up my mind that if Mario wasn't up to the task, I would record the rest of *The Desert Song* selections alone with the orchestra. Then, when and if Mario rebounded, I would bring him into the studio to dub in his voice over the orchestra tracks.

I took one look at Mario and knew that he couldn't do the job that day. Yes, he had been drinking heavily. But it was more than that. He looked drained, used up, a wasted fat man.

I could say nothing to him in front of the orchestra. I could berate him at home, and it would do no good. I could only hope that Mario would realize the futility of a recording session that day—that instead of wasting our time he would bow out gracefully, without a scene or a fight

I started to work alone with the orchestra. An unforgettably forlorn sight, Mario sat slumped in a chair at the side of the stage. He didn't utter a word the whole time.

After we had played forty minutes, Mario dragged himself out of his seat and shuffled almost absent-mindedly up the steps to the control room. He found a seat there, next to the door, next to Betty.

We kept playing, and once or twice, when I looked over at him in the control room, I could see his face buried in his hands, his fingers occasionally clutching at his uncombed hair.

Then he got up, waved through the glass partition, as if to tell me everything was all right, and walked out the door.

As they were leaving, Betty turned toward me. "We're going home," she said in a subdued voice.

25. "None of Us Live Forever"

IN THE early hours of the damp August morning, the unconscious form of Mario Lanza lay wet and cold on the marble walk outside his bedroom.

Only hours before he had had a terrible argument with Betty. Cries of anger and pain, violent recriminations and irrational insults filled the air. Then Betty, hapless champion of a cause that had been lost somewhere in the darkness of her own mind years before, had gone to bed in another room.

All night rain beat on the roof of the villa. For most of the night Mario lay in a helpless heap—a pitiful remnant of a man in the Roman rainfall.

When the servants started to stir in the morning, they found Mario. He was rushed to the Valle Giulia Hospital. The doctors said he had pneumonia.

"Do you think he'll live?" I asked when I arrived at the hospital.

"He should recover," they said. "But he's had a close call."

As I waited for them to let me in to see him, I recalled, with a bitter grimace, *Voice in the Mirror*, a movie Mario, Betty and I had gone to see only a few weeks before at the Fiammetta. We went in not knowing what the film was about, but as it progressed I realized with a certain embarrassment that it dealt with alcoholism.

Suddenly Mario nudged me with his elbow and muttered, "Why the hell did we come to see this picture? It's giving me the creeps."

But we stayed and watched till the end. As we left the theater, Mario said, "You won't catch me taking any more of that damn stuff. Never again."

Now, as I remembered that brave promise, I could only feel a chill of resignation. Too late, too late, I thought, for promises. Too late for Mario.

He greeted me with a wan smile. He looked years older than his 38 years.

"Nothing can kill me," he said, but the bravado was forced. "Stop looking so worried, Costa. When I get out of here we'll finish that *Desert Song* and I'll go back on a diet."

Then, for the thousandth time, the freshet of promises flowed: to stop overeating, to stop drinking, to curb his temper—on and on.

Each day I visited him at the hospital. And each day the promises kept flowing from Mario's lips, and plans for the future. He would do more concerts, he would do more movies—he always wanted to do *Laugh, Clown, Laugh*, and a musical version of *Golden Boy*—and he would make some TV spectaculars, he would return to Germany to finish the concerts he had canceled, he would become the world's greatest opera star.

My heart yearned for them all to come true. But my mind, and now my eyes, told me it was impossible.

In a few days Mario left the hospital. He was back on a strict diet. If he wanted to fulfill the movie commitments that loomed ahead, he would have to take 70 or 80 pounds off his bulging frame. He said he'd try. As he moved from one room to another in his villa, he carried a small pail with him in one hand, and a bottle of fiuggi—mineral water—in the other. From time to time he'd take a sip of the fiuggi, but he would never swallow a drop. Instead, he would spit it into the pail. It was gallingly hot that summer in Rome and denying himself water cost Mario a tremendous expense of willpower. Yet I knew that at any moment he would undo it all—and himself—with one glass of beer.

When I arrived each morning to prepare Mario again to finish the *Desert Song* recordings, he pounced on me to tell me how much weight he was losing. Sometimes it was two kilos (four pounds), sometimes slightly more or less. It was clear that some weight was dropping off. But the tax on his heart . . .

The afternoons were crowded with activity, too. Al Panone and Irving Pisor, co-producers of Mario's future films, were constant visitors. Sam Steinman, a publicity man, was usually on hand, too. And Mario greeted them all with his pail and his fiuggi in hand.

Now I started on a process of dubbing, which I had never done before with Mario. With Betty in the control booth, the engineer would play the record from *Desert Song* once; Mario and I would listen intently in the studio. Then the record would be played over again, and this time Mario would sing to it, with me conducting just a few feet away. The third time Mario's voice would actually be recorded. Then we would go to the control room to listen to the synchronization. When we were satisfied with what we'd done, we would go on to the next recording.

We repeated no song more than once. After we had completed two recordings, Mario was so elated by this second-rate technique that he asked me to make all of our future records just this way.

By one o'clock we had finished all the selections of *The Desert Song*. As we ended our work, Mario said, "Now let's have a caviar feast!"

I knew it meant he was breaking his diet, and Betty knew it. But as usual we couldn't stop him, and he wouldn't accept our refusal to join him.

On September 10, 1959, just before I was scheduled to return to the United States for a brief visit, Mario and I recorded *The Lord's Prayer*. He sang the selection with a memorable expansiveness. This was a voice at its best—after everything and in spite of everything.

When we got back to the villa for a bite of lunch, Mario asked me to do something very important for him when I returned to America.

"Get my dad to come over and stay with us," said Mario. Already Mario's mother, Betty's mother, and Mario's grandfather Salvatore, who was deeply loved by both Mario and Betty, had

258

come to live with them. But he wanted his father, too. Tony hadn't come with Maria because the trip seemed too much for him.

"You know, Costa, none of us live forever," Mario continued.

"I'll do what I can with Tony," I promised.

Then I told Mario where I had put all of the scores of the *Great Caruso* album that we were starting to work on. I left my portable record player in a living room closet, and Mario insisted I leave my suitcase in the basement until I returned.

The children lined up for me to kiss them. Then Mario and Betty escorted me to the door.

"We'll see you in six weeks," said Mario. "If you get lonely for us before then, come any time you want."

That was the last time I saw my friend Mario alive.

In the final days of August and the beginning of September Mario was troubled by intense pains in the left side of his chest. The pains had become so persistent and alarming by September 25, just two weeks after I had left Rome, that Mario was taken to the Valle Giulia for further rest and examination. He had a high fever now, too, and the doctors were concerned.

Once in the hospital Mario was a lonely, anxious, embittered man. He had a loyal nurse, Guglielmina Anselma Mangozzi, who watched over him every minute; and his doctor, Professor Guido Morica, did all he could to discover the sources of Mario's illness. But Mario was hardly a good patient. He was anxious to get out of Valle Giulia and back home to Betty, who was then also bedridden and unable to take care of her family.

When Dr. Morica found that Mario's heart was deteriorating from hypertensive heart disease with arteriosclerosis, Dr. Della Torre, a heart specialist, was immediately called in. Dr. Torre took a cardiogram, and after reading the results, decided that it was his duty to warn Mario of his poor condition.

"Continue abusing yourself, and you will not last long," said Dr. Torre. "You must start living a quiet, regulated existence, if you expect to prolong your life."

Mario listened almost impassively While the doctor pronounced his verdict. But as soon as the doctor left the room, he broke into a red-faced, apoplectic rage.

He shrieked at his nurse, Anselma, that he never wanted to see Dr. Torre in his room again. "I'll chase him out with my own fists! He doesn't know what he's talking about, the fool!"

A few days later, on the evening of October 6, Mario complained he wasn't feeling well. But, when Dr. Morica came to minister to his needs, he informed him that he was going to leave the hospital the next day to go home and see Betty and supervise the children.

With the exception of the daily calls he would make to Betty, and a single visit from Mrs. Alfredo Panone, Mario had seen nobody and talked to nobody while he had been in the hospital. He was desperately lonely—and afraid.

Dr. Morica argued that Mario should not leave the clinic for a moment, that he was badly in need of complete rest. He got his way, but only because Mario had drained his physical resources. He had nothing left to fight with.

On the morning of October 7, 1959, Mario spoke briefly and warmly to Betty on the phone. Then he got up from his bed to sit on the couch and read his newspapers. He was in his pajamas and had slippers on his feet.

Suddenly, Anselma heard Mario utter a cry of pain: "Oh, oh!" Then Mario bent slowly toward his left side. Anselma ran to him, heard him whisper in a barely audible voice, "I love you, Betty . . . Betty . . ."

He collapsed on the couch.

Anselma rang the bell and the staff rushed into Mario's room. Dr. Morica moved Mario onto the bed swiftly and immediately began working Mario's arms in a vigorous battle to keep life in my friend.

His struggle was in vain.

Mario Lanza—the man who had become the American Caruso—was dead.

THE MARIO LANZA DISCOGRAPHY

Courtesy of RCA Victor Records

CATALOG NO.	TITLE
*10-1561	*Be My Love*
*49-1351	*I'll Never Love You*
*10-1582	*O Holy Night*
*49-1888	*The Virgin's Slumber Song*
*10-3207	*Because*
*49-3207	*For You Alone*
*10-3208	*My Song, My Love*
*49-3208	*I Love Thee*
*10-8228	*Vesti la giubba*
*49-8228	*Ave Maria*
*10-3300	*The Loveliest Night of the Year*
*49-3300	*La donna è mobile*
*10-3435	*Marechiare*
*49-3435	*'A Vucchella*
*10-3738	*Lygia*
*49-3738	*Temptation*
*10-8914	*The Song the Angels Sing*
*49-3914	*Because You're Mine*
*10-3961	*You Do Something to Me*
*49-3961	*Lee-Ah-Lee*
*10-4209	*If You Were Mine*
*49-4209	*Song of India*
*10-4211	*Call Me Fool*
*49-4211	*You Are My Love*
*10-4213	*Granada*
*49-4213	*Lolita*
*12-1106	*O Sole Mio*
*49-0902	*Mattinata*
*12-1192	*Granada*
*49-1169	*Lolita*
*12-3155	*Serenade (Toselli)*
*49-3155	*Serenade (Drigo)*

Discontinued

*12-3209	*Addio alla madre (Farewell)*
*49-3209	*O tu che in seno agli angeli*
*49-3665	*Che gelida manina (Puccini)*
*10-4216	*I'll Walk with God*
*49-4216	*Beloved*
*12-1286	*Oh, Holy Night*
*49-1338	*The Virgin's Slumber Song, Op. 76*
*10-4220	*Golden Days: Summertime in Heidelberg*
*49-4220	*Drink, Drink, Drink*
*10-4218	*Deep in My Heart*
*49-4218	*Serenade*
*10-4224	*Some Day*
*49-4224	*Sylvia*
*ERA-51	*MARIO LANZA SINGS*
ERA-100	*NEOPOLITAN SONGS*
*ERA-110	*MARIO LANZA IN OPERA*
ERA-115	*FOUR FAVORITE CHRISTMAS CAROLS*
*ERA-130	*MARIO LANZA IN MOVIE HITS*
*ERA-136	*FOUR OPERATIC ARIAS*
ERA-222	
*DM-1649	*MARIO LANZA SINGS CHRISTMAS SONGS*
*WDM-1649	
*LM-155	
*DM-7015	*BECAUSE YOU'RE MINE*
*LM-7015	
LM-1837	*THE STUDENT PRINCE*
ERB-1837	
ERA-1-1837	
*DM-1330	*THAT MIDNIGHT KISS*
*WDM-1330	
*LM-86	
*20-6334	*I'll Walk with God*
*47-6334	*Ave Maria (Schubert)*
*20-6478	*Serenade (from the film "Serenade")*
*47-6478	*My Destiny*
*420-0770	*La donna è mobile*
*447-0770	*Vesti la giubba*
*420-0771	*Be My Love*
*Discontinued	

264

447-0771	*The Loveliest Night of the Year*
*420-0772	*Begin the Beguine*
447-0772	*Night and Day*
*420-0773	*Siboney*
447-0773	*Valencia*
*420-0774	*Ave Maria*
447-0774	*The Lord's Prayer*
*420-0850	*First Noel*
447-0850	*Silent Night*
*20-6644	*Earthbound*
*47-6644	*This Land*
*20-6664	*Love in a Home*
*47-6664	*Do You Wonder*
*20-6915	*Behold!*
*47-6915	*A Night to Remember*
447-0776	*Serenade*
	Granada
447-0775	*Drink, Drink, Drink*
	Giannina Mia
*20-7164	*Arrivederci Roma*
47-7164	*Younger Than Springtime*
*20-7119	*Come Dance with Me*
*47-7119	*Never Till Now*
47-7439	*For the First Time*
	O Sole Mia
*ERA-262	*LANZA*
*ERB-65	*THE TOUCH OF YOUR HAND*
LM-1927	
*ERB-67	*THE MAGIC MARIO*
LM-1943	
*ERB-70	*MARIO LANZA IN "SERENADE"*
LM-1996	
ERA-288	*LANZA SINGS CHRISTMAS CAROLS, VOLUME 1*
LM-2029	
ERA-289	*LANZA SINGS CHRISTMAS CAROLS, VOLUME II*
LM-2029	

Discontinued

265

*ERA-1-2090	*MARIO LANZA IN A CAVALCADE OF SHOW TUNES, VOLUME I*
LM-2090	
*ERA-2-2090	*MARIO LANZA IN A CAVALCADE OF SHOW TUNES, VOLUME II*
LM-2090	
*ERA-3-2090	*MARIO LANZA IN A CAVALCADE OF SHOW TUNES, VOLUME III*
LM-2090	
*ERA-290	*LOVE IN A HOME*
*ERA-292	*LANZA ON BROADWAY, VOLUME I*
LM-2070	
*ERA-293	*LANZA ON BROADWAY, VOLUME II*
LM-2070	
*ERA-294	*LANZA ON BROADWAY, VOLUME III*
LM-2070	
*DM-1395	*TOAST OF NEW ORLEANS*
*WDM-1395	
LM-75	
DM-1506	*THE GREAT CARUSO*
*WDM-1506	
LM-1127	
*DM-1417	*POPULAR SONGS FROM TOAST OF NEW ORLEANS*
*WDM-1417	
*WDM-1606	*LOVE SONGS AND NEOPOLITAN SERENADE*
LM-1188	
*ERB-1860	*A KISS AND OTHER LOVE SONGS*
LM-1860	
*EPA-4242	*THERE'S GONNA BE A PARTY TONIGHT*
CAL-450	*YOU DO SOMETHING TO ME*
EPA-5047	*BE MY LOVE*
EPA-5048	*I'LL WALK WITH GOD*
LPM-1765	*BEST LOVED SACRED SONGS, VOLUME 1*
EPA-5071	*OPERA AND OPERETTA*
EPA-5083	*THE LOVELIEST NIGHT OF THE YEAR*

Discontinued

266

61-8505	*Funiculi Funicula*
	Maria Mari'
EPA-4222	*SEVEN HILLS OF ROME*
LM-2211	
EPA-4344	*FOR THE FIRST TIME*
LM-2338	
LSC-2338	
LM-2331	*MARIO!*
LSC-2331	
LM-2333	*LANZA SINGS CHRISTMAS CAROLS*
LSC-2333	
47-7622	*Guardian Angels*
	I'll Walk with God

Printed in Great Britain
by Amazon